# Praise for *When a Toy Dog Became a Wolf and the Moon Broke Curfew* . . .

"This gripping story of survival in Amsterdam during World War II is a tribute to the fiercely courageous mother who keeps her child (the author) and herself alive after her husband is shipped off to a Nazi work camp. Hendrika de Vries writes, 'we were a generation of children raised in war and oppression who learned that people disappeared from their homes, from school, and off the street, and you did not ask questions.' This beautifully crafted memoir reminds us that we are never far from oppression by those who wish to silence us."

—Maureen Murdock, author of *The Heroine's Journey: Woman's Quest for Wholeness*

"Reading Hendrika de Vries's memoir of her childhood in WWII Amsterdam was a real adventure for me, one that stirred up many memories of my own, less traumatic, experience of those years. I am especially impressed by how superbly she communicates both the perspective of the child she once was and of her present self and by her richly detailed memories of the Hunger Winter of 1944 to '45, the absence of the father she loved, and her mother's bravery. She writes honestly, too, of the postwar difficulties for each of them—mother, father, child—when the father returned and they had to rediscover how to be a family once again. Hendrika is a fine, fine storyteller."

—Christine Downing, PhD, scholar and author of *The Goddess: Mythological Images of the Feminine* and *The Luxury of Afterwards*

"A nail-biting tale of female strength, spiritual resilience, and resistance to evil that is relevant today. You won't ⸻ written story."

—Dr. B

at

"DeVries's book is a beautifully told story of the madness and joys circling everyday life in a child's neighborhood in wartime. The vividness of her memories serves to frighten in one moment and nourish the next. In that way her narrative is like a Northern European fairy tale—the old kind: gripping, devastating, and enchanting. Her understanding of the psyche of a family will be fascinating to people working with trauma and family therapies and epigenetic transmission of experience—even though she intentionally never leans on the language of these fields. Her inspiring story speaks eloquently for itself."

—Nor Hall, author of *The Moon and The Virgin:*
*Reflections on the Archetypal Feminine*

"This invaluable memoir is written in the authentic voice of a child but informed by a mature adult sensibility that continues to bring insights as it progresses. It portrays a real-life, 'ordinary' woman who risks her life and her daughter's to hide a Jewish girl who becomes a 'stepsister' in the home. This eminently readable book illuminates the bonds that develop between mother and daughter in wartime, the daily grind of home life under the Nazis, and the devastating consequences of the war even for a family where everyone survives. Don't start it in bed. You won't be able to put it down".

—Mary Fillmore, author of Sarton Women's
Book Award winner *An Address in Amsterdam*

"A riveting memoir of Nazi-occupied Amsterdam as seen through the eyes of a young Dutch girl. A hidden Jewish girl, a Gestapo interrogation at gunpoint, betrayals of neighbors, and near starvation during the Hunger Winter make this harrowing saga a tale of moral choice, spiritual stamina, and resistance that has relevance for our times."

—Patricia Reis, author of award-winning
*Motherlines: Love, Longing, and Liberation*

"From the first page, DeVries's book left me holding my breath at what she and her parents went through when the Nazis took over Amsterdam, one of the worst times in western history. When age five, she lost a comfortable and safe world. DeVries's storytelling makes this nonfiction book read like a good novel. Readers almost 'live' what she and her family experienced, and how they rebuilt their life."

—Susan Miles Gulbransen, book columnist for the
*Santa Barbara News-Press* and *Noozhawk*

"The title of Hendrika de Vries's memoir made me instantly curious about what it could mean; I wondered what myth could be lurking in its folds. But I could not have grasped the fierce pull of the narrative describing her world in Amsterdam from 1942 to 1950, which covers the horrific brutality of the Third Reich in her city and the suffering it engendered in inhuman forms of barbarism. But even more, it relates the astonishing strength of her mother, who kept the two of them alive during horrific conditions of survival, starvation, and then starting over. Hendrika is a master storyteller."

—Dennis Patrick Slattery, PhD, author of *Riting Myth, Mythic Writing: Plotting Your Personal Story,* and *A Pilgrimage Beyond Belief: Spiritual Journeys through Christian and Buddhist Monasteries of the American West*

# When a Toy Dog Became a Wolf and the Moon Broke Curfew . . .

# When a Toy Dog Became a Wolf and the Moon Broke Curfew . . .

A MEMOIR

Hendrika de Vries

SHE WRITES PRESS

Published August 2019
Printed in the United States of America
Print ISBN: 978-1-63152-658-9
E-ISBN: 978-1-63152-659-6
Library of Congress Control Number: 2019934428

For information, address:
She Writes Press
1569 Solano Ave #546
Berkeley, CA 94707

She Writes Press is a division of SparkPoint Studio, LLC.

*In memory of my parents*
*They showed me what strength of character looks like.*

*Memories are the key not to the past, but to the future.*

　　—Corrie ten Boom, Dutch resistance fighter in WWII

# Contents

# Author's Note

This is a work of nonfiction. The events and experiences described are historically true and recounted as faithfully as I remember them; with an acknowledgment that early childhood experiences and often-repeated family stories have a tendency to blend in memory. I have changed some names for the sake of privacy, but have intentionally left others as they still live inside of me. To change them would feel inauthentic and dishonorable. Conversations and dialogues occurred originally in Dutch and have been reconstructed in English from recollections and childhood impressions. They do not represent word-by-word accounts or translations; rather I have retold them in the way that preserves the meaning of what was said and conveys the emotional spirit of our encounters and relationships.

# Chapter 1

# "Remember the Warmth and the Light . . ."

## Amsterdam, October 1944

Y ou are seven years old and have never known your mother to be anything but disciplined and in control, even when interrogated at gunpoint, so why is she suddenly marching through the house flipping on every light switch? Like a woman possessed, she strides with determination from room to room: first into her bedroom where she flicks on the lamp on the dresser and the reading light next to her bed, then into your bedroom where she pushes up the wall switch, and then, with a quick yank, pulls the knobby chain on the white ceramic cat with the crooked lampshade on his head that makes everyone smile. With an abrupt turn, she enters the hallway as you walk behind her, your questions silenced by the grim set of her mouth and the intimidating force of her swinging arms that almost hit your head. Now into the bathroom, after which she stomps into the living and dining rooms to turn on more wall switches, yank chains, and push buttons for ceiling lights and single lamps. *Why is she doing this?* Perplexed, your heart pounding, you follow her into the small kitchen where, striking a series of matches, she lights every single jet on the gas stove, including the oven. With all the gas jets lit and blazing at full power, she places two straight-backed chairs in front of the gas stove and opens the oven door.

"Sit," she orders.

You obediently climb on one of the chairs. She sits on the other close to you. The intense blast from the open oven and flame-shooting gas jets heats your face and the full front of your body.

"I want you to feel this warmth and see all the light and always remember it," your mother says, her eyes locked onto yours, her cheeks reddened from the heat. "We are facing cold, dark days, but I want you never to forget this feeling of warmth and light, and I want you to know that no matter what happens, all this light and warmth will return."

You nod, not at all sure you understand what is going on, but you tell her that you will remember. How can you not? Your face is burning up from the heat, and your home is lit up like a Christmas tree.

The next day the electric power and gas are turned off indefinitely in the city of Amsterdam, which is about to face one of the most brutal winters in its history. More than twenty thousand people will die of cold and starvation in the next five months. The history books of World War II will record this time as the "Hunger Winter."

Seventy years later, you wake up in another part of the world and suddenly realize you are old, but inside your head that curious child spirit still remembers and clamors to make sense out of all the madness we humans create and the choices we make. "What on earth is the meaning of it all?"

And despite achy joints and a need for naps, you go along with this questioning voice and are plunged back into places and feelings you thought had been left behind a long time ago. You remember your grandmother's death, and how you wished she had written down the stories she once wanted to write, and then your daughter's daughter, your granddaughter, tells you that her future children deserve to know how we came to the radical actions and the choices we made in those long-ago days. But how can you make them understand the magic of love, courage, and hope, and the power of the women that you witnessed in that time of great darkness? You find yourself wondering if character can be taught or lives on in great-grandchildren's DNA, and your mind floats back like old driftwood to the gray, far-away shore of your own beginning, which of course you can't possibly remember, but you were told the story.

# Chapter 2

# Back to the Beginning

"Push! Push harder," my grandmother, my father's fierce mother and midwife to women in our working-class neighborhood, commanded my mother, who lay spent from the long hours of labor trying to thrust me out of her body. "Push, push again, push . . . This child does not want to be born!"

And from that often-repeated story, I learned that with one last excruciating push, my mother delivered me in my parents' bed in their two-bedroom apartment on a narrow cobblestoned street in the heart of the old city of Amsterdam.

"You have a daughter," my grandmother said to my father, who was also present at the birth, as she placed my slippery small body in his arms.

To which he is said to have nodded and said, "That's just fine."

I guess I was in no hurry to enter this world. Did my soul know what was to come? Perhaps. I stem from a long line of strong women with uncanny intuitive knowing. The premonition could have come through my motherline in the womb, or maybe my psyche had already claimed my father's imagination and sense of fate. Who knows?

I only know for sure that I fell in love with my daddy the moment I took my first breaths on earth. Those strong arms promised to shield and protect me from a world already teetering on the brink of mass madness and cruelty.

For the first years of my life, I was daddy's little girl and he my undisputed hero in a family that sheltered me within a simple domestic order in which the roles of fathers, mothers, and little girls were clearly defined. Mothers stayed home to manage the household, cook the meals, and care for the children. Fathers ventured out into a mysterious world where they did exciting things like earn money, drive cars, and fight mythical dragons or maybe just "bad people" who wanted to hurt women and children, while little girls like me were groomed to marry a handsome prince and live "happily ever after."

In one of my earliest memories, it was my father who rushed me to the doctor to be stitched up when I bled and screamed bloody murder after cutting my hand on an empty can of the wax my mother had used to polish the hallway floor to a sheen. On the way home he bought me all the chocolate I could eat for being his "brave girl," a title I embraced with pride.

War with Germany, even though the Netherlands had hoped to remain neutral, loomed on the horizon, and my father was called to military service in the Dutch Cavalry, just at the time when I was stricken with scarlet fever in an epidemic that swept through our nation and took the lives of many young children as well as adults. In those pre-antibiotic days, when penicillin was not yet available, scarlet fever often proved fatal. The only available treatment consisted of isolating the patient while waiting out the course of its deadly high fevers. Homes that held a patient diagnosed with the contagious disease were quarantined so that no one could enter; that included my father, who was prohibited from coming home from military service for the six weeks it took for my body to win its fiery battle. It was my mother who sat alone by my bedside, cooled my heated body with cold washcloths, and wet my parched lips with her fingertips, while she prayed for the "miracle" of my survival during those long, dark, lonely nights until the fevers finally broke. I must have been aware that my physical survival depended on her constant vigilant care, and I imagine that I loved my mother. But it was the photo of my father that she had hung above my crib, the photo of the uniformed cavalryman seated tall on his horse in service to his country, that I stared at with blurry eyes and for whose presence I longed and wanted to get well.

My father taught me the gift of natural magic. The burning fevers had ravaged my skin so badly that it peeled off my feet and hands like thin papery socks and gloves. I have been told that I had to learn to walk all over again, and my hands were so sensitive to the touch that it threatened to become a chronic emotional problem. Neither the visiting nurse nor my mother could persuade me to touch a toy or pick up a spoon to feed myself. But when my father was finally permitted to return home, he looked down at my hands and told me with a beaming smile that it was "wonderful" because the new pink skin had brought me "magic."

An amateur photographer, he possessed a 35 mm camera that was always an object of my curiosity, but that I had been sternly warned by my father on many an occasion "not to touch," because it was "not a toy to play with."

But now gently taking my hands in his, he said, "Since your hands have shed that thick old skin and are growing new skin, I think you have a magic camera touch." With that he held the camera between his hands and mine and told me to close my eyes and feel it. Then he added, "I bet your hands have so much magic in them now that you could even change the film."

"No, I don't know how to do that, Daddy," I have been told I reminded him with some indignation.

"Oh, I think you can," he insisted. "Just keep your eyes closed."

Then he proceeded to gently guide my fingertips across the back of the opened camera to feel the film. By the end of that afternoon I had, with his hands patiently moving mine, taken the old film out of the camera and put the new roll in. That evening, still glowing with pride at my accomplishment, I picked up a spoon and fed myself. Trust in my own power of touch had been restored and my belief in natural magic was born.

Of course, had I been an older child, I would also have been aware that at about that same time, in May 1940, Hitler's Luftwaffe bombs had obliterated the center of Rotterdam, my mother's city of birth and the place of residence for her mother and siblings. Close to a thousand people were reported killed and more than eighty thousand, including my grandmother and uncles, lost their homes on the day of that bombardment. But sheltered in my innocent cocoon of childhood where hatred and bigotry did not exist and everyone could still safely walk the streets in freedom, I did not notice my mother's grief and concern for her family in Rotterdam. My father's storytelling continued to wrap me in a mythical world in which magicians, princes, and shape-shifting heroes always kept the world safe for little girls.

My father had a natural gift for storytelling, and oh, how I loved to curl up in his lap and participate in his ability to make the characters in our stories come to life.

"Tell me another story, Daddy!" I clamored at bedtime when he always let me choose which it would be that night: a tale of a mythic hero, of gods or goddesses retold from his own remembered version of the Greek and Norse mythology he loved, a fairy tale from the thick book of the Brothers Grimm, or one of my other favorite stories from the many children's books that lined my bedroom shelf. There were always plenty of books to choose from, because I had been born into a family of readers.

With his strong arms securely wrapped around me, comforted by the familiar smells of his pipe tobacco, and the rubber, wood, and paints with which he worked, my imagination could drift on his deep voice into the magical landscapes of fairy tales and myths where, in my father's version, the good characters always outsmarted the bad ones, magical helpers somehow appeared in time, and creatures could change their shape at will.

"You want to hear the one of that king with the funny name, Kaskoeskilewan, and the two giants again?" he would say, laughing.

"No, no. Tell me about that big old sea lion, Daddy."

"Ah, you mean that old Greek god who can change his shape whenever he wants to?" The chuckle of his delight propelled me into the realm of mythic imagination and possibility that would inform my worldview for the rest of my life.

"You sure now?" he often teased.

"Yes, yes!" I squealed in response, while I hugged a tiny three-by-four-inch faded toy dog. The once-red little dog had been my bedtime companion since birth, as shown by its presence in one of my earliest baby pictures, where it sits stiff and new with the insides of its bright red ears still pristine white, a little bell on a pretty collar around its neck.

The little bell and collar had long since gone, its stuffing flattened, its color faded with time and too much little-girl loving, but it still held the magic of my daddy's story-time world.

"Do you think my little dog can change into something else?" I asked him.

"Of course he can. What do you want him to be?"

"Oh, I don't know. A big bad wolf?"

"How about a big good wolf, a gray wolf that will howl at the moon and protect you from everything."

"From everything and everyone?"

"Yes, of course, from everything and everyone, just like I always will," my father said, as he wrapped his arms around me and made a howling wolf sound that caused me to explode into giggles and snuggle down in the innocent illusion of his omnipotent power.

*My dad in Dutch military service—1939-40*

# Chapter 3

# A Crack in the Paternal Shell

I was four years old before bigotry and cruelty forced the first crack in the protective paternal shell and gave me a glimpse of a world in which not all little girls were safe. That was also the day I recognized, with a confusion I could not yet articulate, that my father's desire to protect also gave him the power to hurt me. A possibility that had not entered my young mind while we shared the imaginary dangers in the fairy tales and stories he read and told, but that pushed itself into my awareness on the cobblestoned street in Amsterdam where he and I had gone for one of my favorite walks.

My parents and I belonged to the walking culture that has always thrived in the heart of Amsterdam. If you grew up in the center of the city in those days, you learned at an early age that your legs were your best friends. An hour or two stroll across town on the weekend, even on a rainy day, was not at all unusual, and normal household management demanded daily walks to various local stores. There was the neighborhood morning ritual when I joined my mother and the other housewives, armed with shopping bags, on their way to buy the supplies for that day's meals. Our afternoon walks took us a little further afield to the local library for the books my parents were always reading, and to the fabric store for my mother's sewing materials. And I recall weekend afternoons and early summer evenings when my parents and I sauntered across town, with an occasional hop on and off the tramcars that crisscrossed the city, for social visits to homes of friends and family. In those days before mobile phones and the Internet created instant communication, personal visits gave my parents a chance to catch up on the latest family news and gossip, and I enjoyed playtime with friends' children and cousins my own age. Every so now and then during the week, my father—I think to give my mother a break—even took me along on one of his regular walks to the neighborhood near the Portuguese Synagogue to visit the homes of Uncles Abe and Jacob, where Aunt Rachel plied me with sweets.

Because I was a girl, the shopping trips on which I accompanied my mother served as initiations into the future of housewife and mother for which my gender at that time in history destined me. Surrounded by the neighborhood women, I learned that each item on that day's menu demanded special consideration. The butcher for the specific cut of beef that my mother would later grind in the meat grinder on our kitchen counter to make the meatballs I loved; the fishmonger for a special filet of fresh fish that my mother fried up for lunch exactly the way my dad appreciated it; then the grocer for coffee, flour, tea, and sugar; and of course, being Dutch, we never missed the daily visit to the cheese shop and the greengrocer with its bins of potatoes and the fresh vegetables in season. But the best stop for me was the bakery with its delicious smell of fresh baked bread just hot out of the oven, which I always got to carry with the promise that a slice of it slathered in butter and jam would be my reward when we arrived home.

The local shops acted as social centers where my mother and the other housewives exchanged neighborhood news and gossip. The shop owners knew most of them by name, and offering a candy, a cookie, or a slice of special cheese never failed to remind little girls like myself that we too would one day follow in our mothers' footsteps. This would be my life, the enclosed world of women, a female realm of mothers and caretakers that would contain me in a comfortable routine and circle of predictability centered on nurture, care, and nourishment.

But when I was allowed to accompany my father on his visits to the homes of Uncles Jacob and Abe, I felt different, special somehow. With my small hand nestled securely in his much larger one, I would ever so carefully measure my footsteps to my dad's, right foot to his left foot, left foot to his right foot, as we walked the many blocks from our home to the Jewish neighborhood where the uncles lived.

"Uncles" Jacob and Abe were not really uncles by blood, but my father's connection with them ran deep. They had befriended one another in the gatherings of entrepreneurial merchants and craftsmen that met regularly in the open market square not far from the synagogue to display their latest inventions or wares. My father owned a small rubber goods manufacturing business that had achieved a status of some success. He had designed a rubber binder that could fasten luggage more securely on the growing number of bicycles in the Netherlands and also secure the bedding on the Murphy or wall beds that were gaining in popularity. On market days when he and the other men operated their stalls, they often brought along their wives and young children. This created a communal spirit and a kind of extended family, in which we small children experienced a sense of both freedom and safety as we roamed and played under the watchful eyes of the many "aunties" and "uncles" who affectionately looked out for us all.

At the homes of either Uncle Jacob or Uncle Abe, the men gathered in the cozy living room crowded with comfortable deep chairs and heavy Dutch furniture or sat around the dining room table. In the traditional style, a heavy plush tablecloth that was more like a

Persian rug covered the table on which stood the china cups and saucers for tea or coffee and the glass ashtrays for the inevitable cigars and cigarettes. Uncle Jacob's wife, Aunt Rachel, and the other women usually socialized in the kitchen, while I sat securely ensconced on my father's lap. I nibbled on a cookie or sucked a sweet candy and inevitably dozed off to the buzz and rhythm of the male voices sharing stories, laughter, and serious conversation. Every so now and then, Aunt Rachel might come in to fill a tea or coffee cup, hand me another sweet, and ask if I wouldn't rather join her and the other women in the kitchen, but I always shook my head no. I liked being the girl on my father's lap in that room filled with deep masculine voices that lulled me into a sleepy sensation of being safe and secure in the world of fathers and uncles, the alluring other world of the men.

Then one day the visits came to an abrupt end. I always knew my dad to be a stern but gentle man who was never mean or hurtful, except for that one time on this particular day. We were out on our usual walk to visit the uncles, my hand as always safely clasped in his, when our approach to their neighborhood was blocked by a group of people. They had gathered on the sidewalk to watch an activity that was taking place on the street just ahead of us. We drew closer, and as I peered out past the legs of the adults, I saw something that I would vaguely recall in later years as a blurred image of people with suitcases. They were being ushered out of an apartment building and pushed into the back of a large, green-colored truck.

But within that unfocused scene, I would always recall with startling clarity the figure of a small girl among them. She was a girl about my size and age, or perhaps a little younger. I heard her scream and saw that she was crying because she had dropped her rag doll on the street, and since she was being dragged toward the truck, she could not turn back to recover it. I spotted the doll where it lay abandoned on the pavement and, trying to squeeze past the adults that blocked my way, I pulled my hand out of my dad's so that I could run over and pick the doll up for that little girl. Instead, I was jerked backward. I recoiled with the shock of a searing pain that shot through my shoulder. My father had grabbed my hand tight and, with a rough and painful grip on my arm, he pulled me hard toward him.

"Daddy, ouch, ouch!" I cried out loud, holding my shoulder in pain, but when I looked up at him, the grim set of his mouth and the anger in his eyes shocked me into silence. He lifted me off the ground, and enfolding me in his arms with my face pressed hard into his neck and shoulder, he turned away from the crowd and carried me the long walk home without uttering a word.

It was the first and only time I remember my father ever hurting me physically. An awareness of something dark and confusing disturbed my childhood innocence that day, an experience of a frightening world in which my beloved daddy had hurt me. Did he want to protect me? Was he afraid that I would be put in the truck with that other little girl? I don't remember ever asking him those questions.

I was a little girl who loved having dolls and stuffed animals around her. Because I was an only child, my dolls were my imaginary siblings. For my second birthday my dad had even bought me a doll that was as big as I was. For months I dragged her around as if she were a twin sister. But on that fateful day, I had my first awakening to a world where little girls were stuffed into trucks and cruelly separated from their dolls. I did not understand how this could happen on my favorite outing to visit Uncles Jacob and Abe, who always made little girls like me feel special and important. My brain was not yet developed enough to grasp what was happening on the streets of Amsterdam that year, but for the rest of my life I would carry the visceral memory of that shock of confusion and the image of that little girl crying out for her rag doll that lay abandoned in the street.

That night, when my father told me my usual bedtime story, I asked him what was going to happen to that little girl who had been dragged from her home and loaded into a truck. He said that the little girl would be all right. I should not worry, and he retold his version of one of my favorite fairy tales in which the "bad people" are punished and the good, kind prince rescues and marries the helpless young princess, who then of course lives "happily ever after."

Then he put his arm around me in a hard hug and assured me, "I will never let anything bad happen to you."

I did not have the awareness yet to ask the question, "Why her and not me?" That would come many years later.

And when my mother came to tuck me in and kiss me goodnight, she told me to remember the little girl in my prayers. "God will take care of her," she promised me.

From that moment on, my father no longer took me with him on his visits to Uncles Abe and Jacob, and in my parents' conversations with each other, I now began to hear the words *resistance* and *hiding* in ways that I did not yet comprehend. When I asked my mother, she told me that the uncles and Aunt Rachel had gone to England where the queen now lived, and I was not to worry. They were safe. I did not yet know to ask my mother, "Safe from what or whom?" For a little while longer, the cracked but still protective cocoon of my parents' love managed to contain my confusion and keep the shattering reality of the hatred and bigotry that had invaded our land outside the walls of our home.

Encouraged by the bedtime fairy tales I had absorbed on my father's lap, my imagination now began to create its own stories in which the little girl and the doll were reunited and "the bad people who drove the truck" were punished like the bad king or queen in the Brothers Grimm's tales. I recall even now that the reunions in my made-up versions were always joyful and the punishments severe. I also said my prayers to God, the Father in Heaven, in the way my mother had taught me, and I lingered just a little longer in that precious childhood fantasy world where kind and powerful fathers, both personal and transcendent, protected all little girls so they could live happily ever after.

*Matching steps with my dad—1942*

# Chapter 4

# Facts, Magic, and Imagination

B eing a child, I could not anticipate the events that were about to assault our family and set me on the path of the woman I was to become.

My mother developed severe abdominal pains. She did not talk about it much, but I often saw her put her hand on her belly and grimace. My always-active mom now spent the afternoons reclining in a comfortable chair or lying down on her bed. One day in early June of 1943, she told me that she would soon need to go to the hospital for an operation to take away her pain and make her well again.

Since my birth she had been the stay-at-home mother and housewife who always took care of my dad's and my needs. I had never even considered the possibility of her going anywhere for herself. Suddenly scared, I told her that I did not want her to go. She explained that the operation was important and reassured me, "Daddy will take care of you while I am gone. You and he can come visit me in the hospital together."

Hearing that my daddy would take care of me eased my fear. I liked that he and I, the two of us, would visit her in the hospital. I was also happy that my mom's pain would go away.

On one of the days that remained before her scheduled surgery, my mother and I were enjoying the peaceful stillness of the sunlit living room of our apartment. We were each absorbed in our own silent task, when the shrill sound of the front doorbell pierced the quiet tranquility of that fateful afternoon. I dropped the piece of the jigsaw puzzle I was working on, while my mother put down her sewing and walked slowly through the hallway to the front door. She returned to the living room with a slip of paper in her hand. Her arm outstretched toward me, she collapsed in my father's favorite green armchair and whispered, "Daddy is not coming home."

*Wait a minute!* She had just a few days ago told me that my dad was going to take care of me while she went to the hospital. *Now she said that he was not coming home?*

Confused, I repeated the words I had heard—"Daddy is not coming home?" I tried to grasp what she meant.

"We are allowed to go and say goodbye to him. We have to pick up his clothes." My mother's words came at me way too fast.

I watched her wipe the tears off her face with the back of her hand.

*Goodbye? Pick up his clothes? What was she saying? Why was she crying?*

My head exploded with questions that I wanted to scream at her, but the only words that managed to come out of my mouth were: "When is he coming back?"

She did not know. "It could be a long time. We have to be strong."

She looked away and said softly, "We have to take a train to see him before they take him away to a camp in Germany. We are lucky— we are allowed to say goodbye."

Her words streamed like rushing water past my ears. *Take a train . . . take him away . . . a camp . . . in Germany? Lucky?* I did not feel lucky. I was still only five years old; my mind could not digest what she was telling me, and I felt like throwing up. I desperately needed her to slow down and hold me, but she hurried me along to my bed-room to put on my shoes and coat.

On my bed the huge pile of stuffed animals and dolls that were my imaginary siblings and friends greeted me with their welcome silence. I fell facedown on top of them and, with my arms stretched out wide to hug as many as I could, I pressed my face and body into their familiar textures and smells. *Why were we going to pick up my daddy's clothes and say goodbye? How come he did not need his clothes? Why was he not coming home?*

My mind was racing with unanswered questions, when my hand clasped around the tiny stuffed animal that always accompanied my dad and me in our bedtime storytelling rituals. I held the little red dog that could become a gray wolf. Suddenly everything became very still. Whether the stillness came from my mind or the air around me I was never sure, but I would into my adult days recall with astonish-ing clarity that at that moment I saw and felt my father's presence as if he were there in the room with me. At his side I saw a large gray wolf. I felt no fear, for I knew that it was the good wolf, the guardian pro-tector in our shared story-time world. Then, whether in my mind's eye or in the room, I saw the wolf change into the little red dog and back again into the gray wolf. Somehow, they slowly merged, so that I could see both the wolf and the little red dog and knew they were one and the same. With a certainty beyond my years but supported by my whole being, I knew in that instant that I needed to get my little toy dog to my daddy. It was very important. And, as if in response to a sacred command from an ancient depth, I stood up and slid the tiny red dog with ritual care into my coat pocket and put on the coat. I was ready to go.

"It's time to leave for the train station, Henny. We need to hurry." My mother's voice broke the silence.

For some reason I would never be able to recall the train ride to the transit camp in the town of Amersfoort from which Dutch prisoners of war were being transported to labor camps in Germany, but I will always have a clear memory etched in my mind of my mother and I inside the camp as we walked toward a high barbed-wire fence that stretched out on either side of us around a group of ugly buildings.

Uniformed guards carrying rifles marched us to a section where the barbed-wire fence was so high that I had to stretch my neck to see the top of it. On the other side of the fence stood my dad facing us. I noticed right away that he was not wearing his own clothes but was dressed in a strange, baggy, gray-colored uniform. *So that's why he did not need his clothes anymore.* I wanted to run over to him, as I always did when he came home from work. I wanted to have his strong arms lift me off the ground, so I could put my arms around his neck and feel his bristly skin against my cheek, but the barbed wire between us created an impassable barrier that we were not permitted to cross. We could see and hear each other, but we could not touch. When my dad stepped closer to the fence and in his deep guttural Dutch voice told me to "be a brave girl for Mommy," my hand tightened around the little toy dog in my coat pocket.

I heard him tell my mother that the war would be over soon. "I'll be home before you know it."

I wanted to cry, but the tears gathered in a hard ball in my throat and prickled behind my eyes. I took the tiny red dog out of my pocket and held it out to him. "He wants to be with you," I whispered. Then, making my voice louder so it could carry the distance through the barbed wire, I said, "Remember? He's the wolf. He will take care of you."

My dad gave me one of his special smiles where his blue eyes told me without words that he loved me very much. The shell around my ball of tears wanted to burst open, but I could not let it. I needed to find a way through the barrier to give my dad the toy dog that he and I alone knew to be a wolf in disguise, a good wolf, a guardian protector. My father nodded his head and pointed to the guard in

German uniform who stood on my side of the fence, then told me to give it to him.

I placed the faded toy dog with its worn skin in the hands of the tall German. "It's for my dad," I stressed and pointed him out through the barbed wire.

The guard glanced at my dad on the other side of the fence and nodded.

But I was not sure that he realized the importance of my request, so I added in my louder voice, "It is very important."

The German guard opened his hand and stared for a moment at the worn, stuffed little toy dog I had handed him. He looked back at my father, then, unexpectedly, bent down to my level, brought his face close to mine, and nodded his head in a slow serious yes.

I felt reassured. I think he got it!

My mom smiled and took my hand. I had not told her about my little dog turning into a wolf that would protect my daddy, and she never asked. As the German guards ushered us off the grounds, I turned around to see my father through the barbed-wire fence. He was walking away from us in his baggy new clothes that had the large letters *KG* marked across his back.

I asked my mother what the letters meant. "They are the first letters for Kriegs Gefangener, the German word for prisoner of war," she said.

Then she and I walked back to the train station without any further word, while I tried to figure out what it meant to be a prisoner of war. I did not want to ask my mother any more questions. Unlike my dad, she had a habit of trying to make me understand things with facts and explanations that sometimes overwhelmed me. Besides, I could feel her sadness through my skin, and from the way she squeezed my hand I knew that she was trying not to cry. Or maybe it was my own sadness, and I was trying not to cry. I really was not sure who was who anymore. She gave me the window seat on the train ride back to

Amsterdam and sat next to me, our bodies touching. It would be just the two of us now.

As the train rumbled through the flat Dutch countryside, my mother said in a firm voice, "Daddy will be all right, you know. He will come back to us."

I didn't feel reassured. After all, she had also promised that he would be home to take care of me when she went to the hospital, and when I didn't answer, she added, "You must always remember that there are good people in the world," and patted my hand.

"When I was a little girl like you, there was also a terrible war. I was about the same age as you are now," my mother said and started to tell me about the time when she was a little girl.

I asked her if her daddy was also a prisoner of war.

"No," she said, "but it was a really, really bad war. A lot of brave soldiers died. And because of that, some good men decided that there should be a law to protect prisoners of war like Daddy."

Then she told me that those good men had met in a place called Geneva, in Switzerland, and that Switzerland was a very beautiful country with high mountains, big lakes, and lots of snow. My mother knew that I liked snow, because in the past winter when the snow had piled up on the square near our home, she and I had started a snowball fight with my dad that made us laugh so hard that we all rolled one another in the snow till we were covered in it. Shivering with cold, the three of us had hurried home and drunk big cups of hot chocolate to warm ourselves. It had been a happy time.

I tried to pay attention to her words, while I imagined high snowy mountains of which I had only seen pictures and wondered if the men she was talking about also threw snowballs with their little girls. In later years she told me that I just asked her, "What did the men do?"

My mother then on that train ride tried to explain the Geneva Convention and the concept of prisoners of war to me, her still five-year-old daughter, in a way that she thought might give me comfort. I learned that soldiers who were imprisoned by the enemy were called prisoners of war. And because soldiers are brave people no matter which country they serve, those good men in Switzerland decided to make a law that said that they had to be cared for properly when caught. "So," my mother explained, "because those good men made that law, we know that the Germans have to give Daddy and the other prisoners of war enough to eat to stay alive and take care of them till the war is over."

I have been told that I argued and questioned, "But he cannot come home?"

She agreed but insisted, "No, but that's why we were able to say goodbye to Daddy and why I know that he will be safe."

She patted my hand again and then informed me that, because we now did not have my dad to take care of us, it was important to learn about laws and make contact with good people whom we could trust and who could help us be strong. She thought she would contact the International Red Cross.

"The Red Cross people take care of soldiers who are hurt in the war, and they also help their families. They will help us too," she concluded, and her voice trailed away as if talking to herself and no longer addressing me.

My young mind still could not grasp everything she had been saying, but I had seen pictures of the Red Cross that helped people, and I felt somewhat reassured by my mother's words. Besides that, my mother had a habit of making sure that I did not forget the things she told me, so I knew she would be sure to explain it again, which she did.

In time I would get used to and even appreciate my mother's way of sharing facts and information as if I were a much older child, and the Geneva Convention as an important step in human justice managed to stay imprinted on my mind well into my adult days, when other wars and laws for the human rights of those who fought them would once again demand global attention. But on this day my mother and I rode the rest of the way in silence, as the train continued to transport us back to Amsterdam in the setting darkness.

I thought of my daddy smiling at me behind that high barbed-wire fence and I hoped that the German guard had kept his promise to give him my little red dog. It would remind my daddy how much I loved him, and I believed with absolute certainty that it could change into the magical gray wolf, the invisible guardian that would bring him home safe.

# Chapter 5

# The Kindness of Strangers

The imprisonment of my father had brought the stark reality of the war into our own home and turned me into an immediate problem for my mother.

"I am so sorry, Henny," she kept repeating, "but the doctor says I cannot postpone my surgery any longer. Now that Daddy is not here, we must find somewhere for you to stay while I am in the hospital."

I didn't quite understand why that should pose such a problem. We had lots of relatives and friends in Amsterdam, many within walking distance. *Surely, I could stay with one of them?*

As a child, I was not yet aware of the grotesque metamorphosis that can happen overnight in a society besieged by hatred and bigotry, but children of war must grow up quickly and adapt to the world of distrust and survival that shatters their innocence.

I had been born into a society of openness where social life centered round the home, with friends and family spontaneously dropping in on each other. At the beginning of the war, my parents and many of their friends and relatives did not even own a telephone. They communicated at their leisure through relayed messages, handwritten letters, and spontaneous personal visits. I remember accompanying my parents on many of their impromptu social calls to friends and relatives, where I always hoped there would be a girl my age to play with. If there was no one at home, a handwritten note served as a notice that the visitors would be back some other time. But as the Netherlands became Nazi-occupied territory, the enemy moved among our midst, and spontaneous visits with open communication grew less acceptable or safe. Where once homes were seen as welcoming dwellings where people gathered to socialize and celebrate life, they now turned into places that held dangerous secrets with life-threatening consequences.

Hitler's thugs and henchmen had rounded up large numbers of the Jewish inhabitants and transported them to the camps in Germany, but they continued their meticulous manhunt for those who had found a place to hide as well as those who had hidden them. In addition, with Germany's young men serving the military might of the Third Reich, Hitler needed slave labor for his factories. Able-bodied Dutch men between the ages of sixteen and forty, or sometimes even older, were now routinely taken captive in the streets and in their homes in order to be sent to labor camps in Germany. Many men went into hiding in their own homes or found shelter with friends and even strangers. The random raids, or "razzias," as they were called, had created a culture of distrust and secrecy where once there had been hospitality and openness.

Survival for increasing numbers of people in Amsterdam depended on the willingness of others to turn their homes into hiding places that, if discovered, put their own lives and those of their family at risk. A life-and-death need for secrecy hindered open communication even among family members and close friends. Many of the men in my parents' circle of family and friends were within the targeted age group of able-bodied males at risk for deportation to Germany as slave labor. And, of course, many of my parents' friends and business acquaintances were Jewish.

Who knew who might be hiding someone? Or which uncle or friend had left their home and gone into hiding somewhere else? And how could you be sure that the person you spoke with or the child you took in might not slip up and unintentionally betray you? My mother tried to explain to me that she was reasonably certain that one of my uncles was in hiding in his own home to avoid being shipped to a labor camp in Germany like my dad. I would also learn later that an aunt and her husband were hiding a Jewish brother and sister, while another relative for a short while sheltered a young German soldier who had escaped from the German ranks and was trying to make his way to England. An aunt who agreed to take me was called away at the last moment when the home of a member of her own immediate family was bombed. The tyranny of the war had created a need for a new kind of safety, the kind that made us all increasingly dependent upon the kindness and courage of strangers.

At the last moment a neighbor stepped in and offered to have me stay with her family for the two weeks in which my mother would be in the hospital for her surgery and mandated recovery time. I did not know the family very well, but they had a little girl close to my age, named Mia, with whom I had played occasionally. Mia's family lived nearby in a large apartment that covered several floors and boasted a spacious living room with a grand piano. I had only been in their home briefly a couple of times, and it made me glad when Mia's mother told me that I would sleep in Mia's bedroom and share her bed, so that I would not feel too lost or lonely.

"Mia's parents are good solid people," my mother assured me. "They will take good care of you."

She would inform me much later that Mia's father was a member of the local branch of the resistance movement that my dad had signed up with just before Hitler ordered all former Dutch military personnel to be rounded up and shipped off to Germany for slave labor. Mia's parents shared my mother's values, which helped her relax.

But the first night of my mother's hospitalization, I woke up sobbing in the dark strange bedroom from a dream in which I was totally alone and could not find either my mother or my father.

I guess my sobs must have been loud, because Mia's mother came to check on me and see what was wrong.

I looked up at this woman I barely knew and cried, "Am I an orphan?"

She assured me in a no-nonsense manner that reminded me of my mother, which I found comforting, that I was not and that I should say my prayers rather than cry, because I would wake up everyone.

Shaking her head at the doll I clutched against my chest, she admonished me that I was "really too big to sleep with a doll anymore," and then added, "Now be a big girl. You are going to have to be strong for your mother. She is not going to feel so good when she comes home."

But she left the bedroom door slightly open to ease my fear and loneliness, and a few days later she took me to visit my mother in the hospital, so that I could see for myself that I was indeed not an orphan. I was also allowed to take flowers, when I told her that my mother would get better faster if she had flowers.

She asked me, "And how do you know that?"

My response was firm. "I know it because my mom puts flowers everywhere in our home, and she wouldn't do that if they didn't make her feel good." Then mimicking what I had heard my father say from time to time, I added, "My mom doesn't do anything she doesn't want to."

Mia's mother and I walked the many blocks to the hospital where, upon our arrival, a young nurse in white uniform took us down a long narrow corridor that led to the women's surgical ward where my mother was resting in recovery. I had never visited or been in a hospital before and, overwhelmed by the smell of nasty strong soap that caused my nose to itch and made me want to sneeze, I wondered why they didn't put pictures or colors on the gray, bare walls of the dark, narrow hallway. I had thought hospitals were places where people went to heal, but I already knew that my mother could never get better in an ugly place like this.

"Your mother knows how to make any place look beautiful," my dad would always say with admiration in his voice, as he brought home a bouquet of fresh flowers at the end of each week, while she chided him for spending too much money but granted that he had picked the mums or marigolds that she liked.

My mother always made it clear that she was happiest when she could wear and surround herself with the colors of autumn, and she made sure that the framed pictures on the walls in our cozy home depicted scenes and landscapes that brought the warm tones of her favorite season into our living space. Plush tablecloths and colorful bedspreads imbued the rooms with warm hues of orange, yellow, tan, and red, while the intricate patterns on the cushions scattered about our living room showed off her fine needlepoint skills in the same warm colors. A tapestry that covered the entire wall of our small entrance hall depicted medieval ladies and their courtly knights. "To help us remember the French in us," she would say with a smile and give me her version of the history of brave knights and their beautiful ladies. My mother liked to say, "French women really know most about beauty," as she artfully penciled her eyebrows and dabbed herself with her favorite 4711 Eau de Cologne to greet my father when he came home from work each day.

I knew for certain my beautiful mother could not heal in this ugly, foul-smelling place where there was no color. She needed to come home fast.

The nurse warned that we could only have a brief time with my mother because she was still "very weak," and marched ahead of us with brisk steps into a ward where a row of narrow, metal-framed beds stood lined up next to each other against the gray wall on our left. I searched the face of each of the women curled up in the beds. Some smiled at me, but none was my mother. Then I saw her. She lay propped up against a couple of pillows in the last bed at the far end of the ward beneath a window. I was glad that she had a window to look out of in this horrible room, but I hesitated. She looked so different, so very small, pale, and helpless in a white gown with her short brown hair pinned behind her ears, but then she stretched out her arms to me and gave me her big *I am so happy to see you* smile. I ran over to her and flung myself on the bed.

She winced. "Ouch, we will have to be a bit careful." She explained that she had a very large cut through the center of her belly and would not be able to pick me up or hug me too tight for a while, but she assured me that she would definitely come home in a week. Mia's mom had been right. I was not an orphan.

My mother whispered in my ear that I should not forget to thank Mia's mom for taking care of me. I nodded yes, but when it came time to say goodbye, I had to squeeze my eyes hard to push away the tears that wished my daddy were here to take me home.

As Mia's mom and I left the hospital and were about to cross the street, a tall German soldier suddenly stepped in front of us with a commanding shout of "Halt!" With a threatening manner he put up his large hand so that it almost touched Mia's mom's face and blocked our passage; then shouting louder, he ordered us and several other people who had stepped off the curb to get back and wait. At that moment, I heard the sounds of the parade of German soldiers approaching us from a distance. With military precision they marched in formation down the middle of the street, their rifles held against their shoulders, ready to aim and fire. The stomping footfall of their heavy boots caused the ground under my feet to shake, and the harsh, rough noise of their thunderous German marching song hurt my ears. I wanted to put my hands over my head and run away, but Mia's mom held my hand in a tight grip as my dad had done in the past. I moved closer so that I could feel the length of her body pressed against mine. She squeezed my hand. My mother was right. I would have to thank her, but I could also feel the tears prickle behind my closed eyelids. The ground continued to tremble. I was grateful for Mia's mom, but I missed my daddy so very much.

*My beautiful mother—1943*

# Chapter 6

# Sounds of Defiance

Groups of German soldiers in shiny polished black boots, pistols tucked in their belts and their hands ready to shoot into the air with an intimidating "Heil Hitler" salute, now appeared on every street corner of our neighborhood. Or maybe I was just noticing them more, since upon her release from the hospital, my mother, who had been a national champion runner and speed walker in her youth, insisted that we take brisk daily walks along the canals to increase her strength. We also began to spend a great deal more time with Mia's family and the people who gathered regularly in their home.

Our own apartment felt empty and lonely without my dad's jovial storytelling presence and the voices of his friends who used to stop by for a cup of my mother's strong coffee or a glass of my father's favorite port wine. In the evenings I missed the sounds of the radio that my father had tuned to receive Radio Orange, the Dutch-language radio program broadcast from the BBC European Service in London, to which he, my mother, and others had listened. Named for the color of the monarchy, the program in which Queen Wilhelmina regularly urged her citizens to be brave and courageous was broadcast by the

Dutch government in exile in London to the occupied Netherlands for fifteen minutes each night.

As a cavalryman in the Dutch Military Service, my dad had once ridden with the queen, a story he loved to relate and that no doubt became more colorful with each retelling, but the fact was that he admired her strength of character with its particular brand of Dutch fortitude and honesty that inspired him and so many others. It was her deep capacity to engender strength and courage that made the radio broadcasts so important to her citizens and therefore dangerous to the enemy.

But to own a radio in Nazi-occupied Amsterdam was now deemed an illegal subversive act punishable by death, and since his imprisonment in Germany, my father's radio receivers had remained silent and hidden. One was stored behind a wooden façade in the back of a kitchen cabinet, the other high up above a bedroom closet with linens and blankets, at least for now.

In contrast to our silent little apartment, Mia's home felt like a multi-storied, welcoming oasis where adults gathered to converse and express their opinions, hopes, and fears, while we children were given enough space to roam and play games, to just be children. As if in defiance of the dark forces of hatred and brutality that stalked the streets and contaminated the air we breathed, the adults gathered around the grand piano in Mia's parents' living room and harmonized their voices in songs of joy and freedom during the lingering daylight hours of those last summer days. The music and songs put smiles on their normally stern faces, defiant smiles that forced hope to dance through the air on the sound waves of the human voice.

My mother, who loved to sing and had a good singing voice, called these evenings "moments of grace." She was not happy if I demanded her attention during those precious gatherings around the piano, and if I persisted, I was certain to get a severe talking to on the walk back to our home. In the lecturing way she had when conveying her truths, she impressed upon me that moments of joy and laughter were "gifts from God" that needed to be treated with respect and were not to be interrupted by a "whiny little girl." It would have been less painful if she had just told me to be quiet. At least I would not have had God to deal with also. But her lessons stuck.

There were times when the adults stretched out their discussions about freedom and the enemy well into the evenings and sometimes the night, when we children were put to bed at Mia's place and the tone of the gathering changed. If we could manage to stay awake, which I sometimes did, we might hear the adults whispering in low serious tones about the course of the war and the Nazi oppression. The word *resistance* floated through the air like a repetitive note in a somber but popular refrain.

This was when Mr. Sleumer first appeared in my life. A tall, gaunt, older gentleman—a lot older, I thought, than either Mia's dad or my own—who addressed everyone with the formal "U" (the Dutch formal version of the informal you), and always dressed in a suit and tie, he intimidated me at first. My mother told me that he reminded her of her own father, the gentlemanly grandfather I had seen in photos but had never known, but to whom she had felt very close until he died when she was only nineteen. She also said that Mr. Sleumer had traveled to many countries and was doing "important work."

I asked her, "What?"

She said, "He can't really talk about it. It has to do with the war, Henny."

And that was the end of the conversation.

But since I could never leave unanswered questions alone, I asked my friend Mia, who whispered that her mother had told her that his work was "something to do with diamonds," but we were "not to ask about it."

And so Mr. Sleumer remained a bit of a mysterious figure. Whenever he joined the growing gatherings at Mia's parents' home, he made it a point to ask me questions about myself. And when he learned that I was curious about other countries, he began to bring me stamps from exotic nations all over the world. He even brought me an album and tried to get me interested in stamp collecting. He also smoked cigars and would hand out the colorful paper cigar bands to the boys, but when I told him that I also liked the bands, he included me in his recipients. The boys thought that was weird since I was a girl and only men smoked cigars, but I could not see why they should be the only ones to collect the interesting bands.

My mother, in the meantime, continued to make sure that she and I took our brisk walks a little further each day. But whenever I saw a German soldier approach us on our side of the street, I wanted to cross to the other side, at which time she would grab my hand and admonish me, "You must not let them make you afraid."

I was not entirely sure if I was afraid or learning to hate, but I knew for certain that I did not want to share the sidewalk with them. However, my mother insisted, "Just walk on and look away from them."

One day my mother decided out of the blue that she felt strong enough to take a longer walk back to the neighborhood near the Portuguese Synagogue and the market square where my father and Uncles Abe and Jacob had met, but when we arrived in the vicinity of the old Jewish area, we were confronted by rolled, barbed-wire barriers and warning signs that cordoned off the streets. Through the barriers we could see that the homes on the streets where I had walked with my father stood mostly empty now, the traffic of German trucks loading up household goods the only visible reminder of the inhabitants who had lived there. This once-vibrant neighborhood of our city had become a ghost area, a dead zone guarded by heavily armed German soldiers.

One of the soldiers motioned us to move on.

My mother gave a deep sigh and remarked on our subdued walk

home, "They are right, those who have survived are now probably in hiding or searching for a place."

I did not know how to respond. It didn't sound like she was really addressing me anyway, more like the way she talked with the adults at Mia's place, so I stayed quiet in my own feelings of sadness and how much I suddenly missed my daddy again.

Not too many nights later, I heard her take my dad's radio receiver out of its hiding place from behind the false cabinet wall in the kitchen. Pretending to be asleep, curled up under the blankets in my bed with my dolls and stuffed animals, my ears picked up the familiar static and the British-sounding announcements. I realized that she was breaking the Nazi law. It was dangerous. I wanted to get up and question her, but I guessed she was listening to the voice of the Dutch government in exile, maybe even the queen herself, the way she and my father had when he was still at home with us. I did not want to interrupt her. Soothed somehow by the familiar sounds of the radio and the thoughts of my father, I must have drifted asleep.

When I awoke the next morning, I told my mother I had heard her listen to the radio and questioned her about disobeying the law. She told me she had decided that it was important for us to know what was happening with the war.

"But it is dangerous," I confronted her.

She agreed, and then sat me down for one of our "grown-up" talks in which she focused this time on a danger that she thought was more threatening to us than listening to the radio. I vaguely recall her telling me that it was dangerous "not to have information," or something to the effect of "the danger of ignorance," or maybe she said that later, as she tried to explain to me in different ways "the risk of not knowing what is going on."

I may not have comprehended my mother's exact words, but I understood the feeling of "not knowing what is going on," because I had experienced that felt sense of confusion and could never tolerate it very well. I think that's why I enjoyed doing jigsaw puzzles where I was in charge of creating a picture out of the jumbled pieces. So my mother had my attention. And I would always remember how hard she worked at trying to make me understand in her factual way that the Nazis wanted to keep us afraid and make us feel helpless so we would not do anything to stand up against them. "Listening to the radio gives us information about other people, such as our friends and neighbors in the resistance movement and the Allies in other countries who are fighting for us, and that makes us stronger," she explained to me patiently until she thought I understood. And I think I eventually did.

"The Nazis do not want us to feel strong," she would often repeat in the weeks and months that followed, "and that is why they do not want us to have newspapers or listen to the radio."

My mother's lectures took deep root in my psyche in those early years. Never one for fantasy or mythology, she preferred history and newspaper facts, and exhorted me, before I even knew the meaning of the word, that I should always read biographies when I got older, and of course newspapers.

"What are biographies?" I remember once asking her, my mind swimming in a sea of information.

"They are the stories of people's lives that help you understand how people make important decisions," she replied.

And so I began to learn at age six from my mother that people's stories are important and information is power. Of course, as I grew older, I would expand that knowledge into an understanding that tyrannical rulers and governments suppress the freedom of the media for that very reason, but at the time I just felt convinced that my mother had a good reason for listening to the radio, even though the Nazis told us it was against the law. It made me feel strong.

# Chapter 7
# A "Normal" Existence

The war would bring new challenges of which I was yet only dimly aware, but for a brief period, my mother succeeded in creating a reasonably normal existence for us. The time had come for me to start school, and since I was an only child, she had decided on a nearby Christian school with small classes so that I could "make friends and learn about God." Even though we had never attended church, and my mother's belief in dreams, omens, and oracles—not to mention her almost infallible female intuition—would horrify the most liberal minister of that time, she continued to draw strength from the God of the Protestant Christianity in which she had been raised as a child. She wanted me to have that same benefit.

I proudly sent my father the photo that was taken of me when I enrolled in my new school. It portrays a girl with squared shoulders, a determined set to her mouth, dark eyes, and a huge starched ribbon on her neatly combed short hair. I was pleased with it and hoped that it would show my daddy that I was being the "brave girl" he wanted me to be.

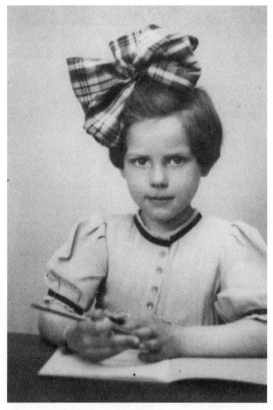

*My first school photo—Sept. 1943*

Through the unwavering support of the International Red Cross, we still received occasional letters from my father. They contained no real information, since most of the words and even whole sentences were blackened out, censored, sometimes even the whole letter. But at least there was his name, and at times the word *love* was left intact. We also received a series of photos showing him and other prisoners looking well fed to prove that, in accord with the Geneva Convention, my father and the other prisoners of war were still being treated humanely. Several photos even showed the men engaged in the sport of boxing. I treasured those photos because they helped fill in the fading picture that I held of him in my heart.

"He is alive, the war will end, and he will come back to us," my mother reassured me, and I believed her.

I knew that she missed my father as much as I did. Sometimes I saw her stroking the credenza that he had built, and when I would catch her in the act, she managed a sad smile and said, "Your dad was always good with his hands. He made all our furniture when we were first married, you know."

I'd nod and we would fall silent. I had no answer because she had told me this several times already. The absence of his powerful presence, his love for stories, his wry jokes, and the friends he brought to the house had left a gnawing emptiness in our home and hearts that neither my mother nor I could fill for one another.

Mr. Sleumer now came to visit us at our apartment occasionally. He continued to bring me stamps from countries that we looked up in an old world atlas my mother had taken out of the glassed-in bookshelves my father had built. I had also begun to paste the cigar bands he had given me in a notebook.

One day, after he had been away on a trip, he brought me some cigar bands that were much larger than the usual ones. He shared with me that these were "very special because they came from cigars that had been smoked by the great Mr. Winston Churchill himself."

Of course I begged for a story, and Mr. Sleumer told me that Winston Churchill was the prime minister of Great Britain, where our queen now lived, and that he was "a great leader who would help us win the war."

I asked him if Mr. Churchill could bring my dad back to us, to which he replied, "I think he can do that, but first we have to win the war."

I decided that I liked that Mr. Churchill, but I was a bit suspicious of Mr. Sleumer being so nice to me. He had told me that I should be very proud of my mother, and I could see how much he liked her. I did not want him to think he could replace my dad, so I would not let him hold or hug me, and I also made sure to tell him that my father had ridden a horse with the queen, so that Mr. Sleumer would not think he was more important than my daddy. But I liked collecting the stamps and cigar bands and had to admit that I enjoyed the way he talked to me as if I were almost a grown-up and not just a little girl.

Being an only child, who spent most of her time in the company of a mother who conversed with me on serious topics as if I were an older confidante, made the transition to being in school a challenge. I was not used to spending all day with children my own age, and I felt anxious and tearful being apart from my mother. So, each school morning presented a drama in which I pleaded with my mother to "please, please, please let me stay home."

My mother tried to convince me that I had "a huge curiosity and a wonderful mind," and there would be "so many things to learn that will be interesting and fun."

I told her I hated the way the school smelled of antiseptic, and I didn't like the girl I was placed next to, and I would "never, ever, ever like it."

And then my mother walked me to the school on the canal several blocks away, and I would hang on to her as she pushed me into the building, where I would stand shivering and sniffling in the hallway until I calmed down or walked out again to where she was always still waiting for me outside the door. We repeated this scenario several times until I fell under the spell of Miss Hoffman, my first-grade teacher, and could not wait to go to school each day.

A religious young woman with a gentle soul, Miss Hoffman brought to the class an imagination and gift for storytelling and drawing that created magical portals into a safe, predictable world of beauty and order where numbers solved puzzles and words were woven into poetry. In childhoods darkened by forces of violence, hatred, and bigotry, she showed us a world of love, where a wise God embraced the earth with its animals, trees and flowers, and all of its little children with infinite kindness.

I absolutely adored Miss Hoffman. She mesmerized our class with her stories and drawings. In her presence, the harsh reality of the war––its pistol-carrying German soldiers who stomped the sidewalks in their heavy boots, its rolled barbed-wire barriers that blocked our streets and neighborhoods, and the barrage of fear and loathing that hung in the air we breathed––was for a short while pushed outside the walls of her protective classroom. For a few hours each day, Miss Hoffman enabled us just to be little children in a gentler environment in which our lessons in reading, writing, and arithmetic were illustrated with stories of kindness and hand-drawn pictures on the blackboard. With her chalked scenes in soft pastels that depicted small children at play amid animals and flowers, she immersed us in a safe and innocent Garden of Eden–like world.

We all clamored for Miss Hoffman to write a personal verse— illustrated, of course, by one of her own sweet drawings—in the little friendship books that we all carried around in those days. It was the custom to invite friends and family to fill a blank page in our album with a verse of poetic wisdom, some words of encouragement, a witty saying, or just a funny ditty that would help us remember them in our later years. Miss Hoffman obliged with a smile but reminded us in her verses "to trust in the Lord and put our faith in God." Her personal verse to me was accompanied by a small pastel drawing that shows a little girl with a watering can sprinkling her flowers. A butterfly hovers above her shoulder.

Dated October 1943, less than a month after I celebrated my sixth birthday, it would be a visible reminder of the warmth, light, and love accessible to the human soul, even as the darkest years of the war still lay ahead of us.

But war abhors tender souls, and one day during class the principal entered the classroom. We all stood at attention, as little Dutch school-children were taught to do in those days. The principal whispered something in Miss Hoffman's ear, and my beloved teacher, who taught us to value gentleness and trust in the loving God in whom she believed, gave a cry of anguish that sounded like a wounded little animal. She burst into soft sobs in front of our class, and as her body collapsed, she was led away by the principal. The class was told that our teacher had gotten sick, but the rumor among the children that some later heard as "a fact" from their parents was that someone close to Miss Hoffman, someone she had loved very much, had been captured by the Nazis.

"Maybe," a couple of the boys whispered, "they have taken Miss Hoffman to a camp also." I did not want to hear that, but I would never discover the truth or see her again.

It was a harsh reminder that the brief "normality" of our innocent first-grade life was an illusion. We were a generation of children raised in war and oppression who learned that people disappeared from their homes, from schools, and off the streets, and you did not ask questions. You were numbed into silence, and you were not old enough yet to understand that the numbness came from the grief that you could not bear to feel.

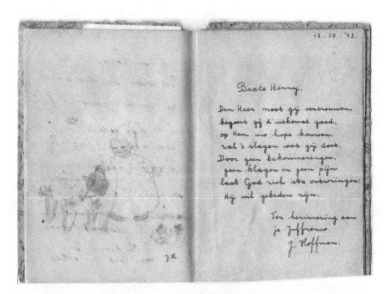

*Miss Hoffman's verse in my Friendship book—Oct. 1943*

# Chapter 8

# Mothers and Daughters

"I think we should go visit Omaatje," my mom announced one morning over our usual bowl of porridge.

"In Rotterdam?" I had not seen my oma—affectionately known by the diminutive of Omaatje, ostensibly because, though large of spirit, my grandmother was small of stature—since before my father had been taken away.

"Yes, it looks like the war may go on for a long time. Things are getting worse. Who knows when I will get a chance to see my mother again," my mom replied.

"You think something bad is going to happen?" I asked in my by-now natural hypervigilance.

"No, I just miss my mother." She shrugged her shoulders as if I, of all people, should understand. As the war dragged on, my mother and I had become a little like an old married couple that read each other's thoughts.

"You must understand," she said, "they say the war could last much longer than we thought, and I want to see my family."

"I'll get to stay with Netty and Loura?" I asked now with some excitement.

Before the war had ruptured the natural rhythm of our lives, the two daughters of my aunt Gretha, my mother's closest sister, had been very much a part of my life. Their dad and mine having been friends before I was born, our families were in and out of each other's lives with frequent visits and extended stays in both Amsterdam and Rotterdam.

On one of their visits to Amsterdam, they had taught me how to skip while they each held on to an end of my skipping rope on the sidewalk in front of our apartment building. My father, always ready to show his pride in my accomplishments, had taken a photo of the three of us from the window above. Of course, that was a long time ago, before he was taken away to Germany. But the thought of seeing Netty and Loura again made me remember the happy times and I liked that feeling.

"Yes, we will stay with Gretha, of course," my mother said, as if I should remember that's what we always did.

My aunt and uncle still lived in the same house where my father had first been introduced to my mother. Their neighborhood had been spared when Hitler's bombs obliterated the historic center of Rotterdam, the city of my mother's birth and home to most of her family at the onset of the war.

"We will visit all your aunts and uncles," my mother added. "It's important for you to know that you have a grandmother and aunts and uncles who could care for you if something happened to me."

"You think something is going to happen to you?" I asked, feeling fearful and suspicious again.

"No, but you have to understand that we are in a war, Henny. We don't know what will happen. I need to see my mother, and I want you to see Oma. She is getting old."

As a child, my mother had not been particularly close to her mother. The youngest of ten surviving children—born within a year of her older sister, a premature baby with severe health problems—she, the healthy one, never felt she had the attention from her mother that she both needed and wanted. But as she grew older, mother and daughter formed a bond around a unique talent. Both my grandmother and my mother had an intuitive gift for prognostic dreaming and an uncanny knowledge of events before they were about to happen. They shared a belief in an existential patterning and order of things that gave meaning to life and placed them in a seamless universe in which dreams, sacred omens, and intuitive guidance moved about easily in ordinary everyday events. A picture would fall, and they would somberly discuss the death that was to follow—and it did. A dream would foretell the birth of a baby girl, or the unknown red-haired man who would come to ask for my aunt's hand in marriage—and it happened.

I gleaned from my mother that which she had learned from her mother, and which I would believe all my life. "The world is always speaking to us. All we have to do is pay attention."

And I learned from them both to take my nighttime dreaming seriously because, as my mother had also been told by her mother, "Our dreams are like angels that guide us through life's difficulties."

Because of their generation, they explained their powerful intuition as a gift from God, but my grandmother also told my mother that it might be because "we are really descended from gypsies."

My girl cousins tried to convince me that we were really "all descended from witches," which for me was the very best story of all.

On the day that my mother and I boarded the train for Rotterdam at the Amsterdam Central station, the platform was crowded with a group of German soldiers who pushed ahead of us to fill up the seats. They seemed to suck all the breathable air out of the cabin with their ultra-loud voices and invasive glances at my mother. I moved my body closer to hers so that we were touching and remained that way for the entire train ride.

The city of Rotterdam still lay in rubble from the bombing from which my grandmother had managed to escape with her life, and we now visited her in the small apartment where she and my gentle, unmarried uncle Dick had made their home. I was not prepared for this tiny, frail old woman, who could not see me very well, to be the same strong grandmother whose image I carried from memory and my mother's stories.

As my mother's relationship with her mother had been formed less in tender love than in mutual recognition and admiration, my mother often shared stories of her mother's strength and courage. I had heard how my grandmother ruled the household when my mother was still a child, a prosperous household with seven sturdy sons and three willful daughters, and servants to boot. My favorite story though was how my grandmother had run away from Hitler's bombs with only her favorite pair of old slippers in her hands, while her house and the city exploded in flames and smoke behind her. In my mind's eye, my oma had been strong and tough, a warrior woman, not this tiny, frail old lady seated in her chair with a pillow cushioning her aching back.

I sat down on the floor with my head at her knees as she leaned forward in her chair and stroked my hair. "You have grown since we last visited," she said, lifting my face up to hers.

I nodded, and she asked me about school. I told her I liked school, especially reading because I enjoyed stories. When she asked me what kind of stories, I found the courage to ask her about running away from the bombs.

She just smiled at me from her near-blind eyes, took my hands in hers, and whispered in a conspiratorial tone, "At least that nasty Herr Hitler did not get my favorite slippers, and my feet are really comfortable." She then pointed to the red geraniums that she was able to grow in her window boxes despite the cold wintry weather. "See those," she said, "they keep on growing, because they are strong, just like us."

That's when I recognized the source of my mother's practical strength, although I would not shape that recognition into formal thoughts and words of wisdom until I was much older, when I would also claim it as mine.

"And they are beautiful," I said to my oma, and I remember that made her smile.

My mother joined us to tell me that my grandmother was getting tired and it was time to go, and we both kissed her goodbye.

Every daughter has her female roots in this primal continuity of her motherline. But the intensity of a close mother-daughter bond, especially when forged in the shared experience of trauma, can mimic a Greek drama that desperately needs some lightening up. And while the visit to Rotterdam gave my mother the opportunity to draw strength and be closer to her own mother, it gave me a chance to get a little distance and breathing room from mine.

Greek mythology in its ever-present wisdom tells an archetypal story about the necessity for levity and differentiation in the mother-daughter bond, even in the face of great loss and suffering. It goes as follows:

The Great Earth Mother Goddess, Demeter, and her only beloved daughter, Persephone, are inseparable. Until one day Persephone is abducted into the underworld by the god Hades, whom she will eventually marry. Utterly distraught at the loss and separation from her daughter, the Mother Goddess abandons herself to her grief, and in a maternal rage ignores her divine responsibilities and even threatens to stop the growing of the grain that supports all life on earth. But in the midst of this intense drama, played out by the archetypal mother and daughter, Greek mythology sneaks in Baubo, an irreverent little female figure who uses bawdy comments and lewd gestures to engage the goddess's sexual imagination and sensual connection to life and earth. Sometimes depicted as just a little vulva, Baubo's earthy humor and irreverent laughter remind the goddess of her own core and purpose and bring her senses back to the earth that needs her attention. Mother and daughter are reunited, but now only for half the year. Balance is restored to the world.

Though admittedly in a somewhat less dramatic way, our visit with my grandmother and my mother's family created a similar rebalance. I spent time in the company of my cousins, while my mother soaked up the familiarity and closeness of her siblings and her own mother, offering both of us a brief respite from the intensity of our mother-daughter relationship. Here amid her large family, I could experience my mother differently from when it was just the two of us. Surrounded by her sister, sisters-in-law, and many brothers, she was less focused on me. I heard her laugh as they bantered, shared risqué jokes, and told each other stories that elicited Baubo-like belly laughs and earthy humor, even as they also shared their collective fears and engaged in serious conversations about the outcome of the war. The sheer numbers of aunts, uncles, and cousins spread the emotional intensity around, so that the close bond between my mother and me loosened a little. She could be more than just my mother; she could be sister, daughter, and playful adversary with siblings' significant others. I could be the child I still was, a little girl with her own destiny and in awe of her fascinating older cousins.

My aunt's two daughters were only a few years older than me, but in my eyes, they already possessed the secrets of womanhood and femininity. I followed them around like a little puppy eager to absorb the older-girl wisdom they shared with pride, laughter, and seriousness. I learned that, as girls, "our bodies are made with a special place inside that is hidden," and that one day, all three of us would be pretty "because both our mothers are pretty," but then I'd "have to watch out for boys." And that led to more serious information such as, "Boys can get very badly hurt if kicked in a certain place," and, "You can't make a baby just by kissing a boy, but you might if you sit on his lap, so you should not do that."

The information they shared felt delicious and, in their young female presence, I discovered that awesome childhood curiosity about my body and being a girl that is still informed by innocence. I forgot for a while how much I missed my father and how often I felt afraid that I might lose my mother, because we were in the midst of a war in which terrible things might happen. Instead, my excitement had been awakened for the wondrous things I had yet to discover about being the girl I was and the woman I might become one day.

As in the Greek myth of Demeter and Persephone, my mother and I had been temporarily reminded that we were separate beings with individual destinies. For a little while, the world was back in balance.

We rode back on the train to Amsterdam with renewed energy, my mother with a smile on her face that gave me a happy feeling. There was a space on the seat between us, and I did not feel the need to move closer to her as I looked out the window at the disappearing countryside.

# Chapter 9

# My Secret Stepsister

"They are winning. We need to fight back. We have to do something!" My mother paced up and down our living room floor shaking her fists in the air.

Mr. Sleumer, who was seated in my father's favorite chair, shook his head. "We need places for families and couples. You don't have anywhere to hide them here."

In their argument, they seemed to have forgotten I was in the room with them. I sipped the tea my mother had made for me earlier. We had not seen Mr. Sleumer for a while, but he had stopped by this afternoon, and my mother was obviously not pleased with him.

"You had told me that they were also looking for places for girls and single women," my mother said, glaring at him.

"Are you sure you want to take the risk?" he replied gently.

"You have someone in mind. I know you do. I know you have been waiting to ask me," my mother said.

"She's a young woman, still a girl really," he said.

"We can make room here for a girl to come live with us." As if suddenly remembering my presence, my mother turned to me and said, "We could do that, couldn't we?"

"Will she be hiding with us?" I asked. Small children have receptive ears and the ongoing duration of the war had made adults less careful in the conversations held in apartment hallways, living rooms, and on the corners of the street. At this stage of the war, it was no secret to children my age and even younger that Jewish people were hiding in homes of friends, family members, and even neighbors in our city in an effort to avoid being captured by the roaming Nazis who wanted to send them to the camps in Germany we had all heard about, and where, we whispered among ourselves, they might be murdered.

"Can't she go to England like Uncle Jacob and Aunt Rachel?" I asked.

"It's too late," my mother said.

Mr. Sleumer stood up to leave. He looked down at me. "You won't be able to talk about her. You have to keep it a secret. Do you think you can do that?"

I nodded, and he and my mother walked to the front door together.

A few days later, a young woman named Nel moved into our home and into my bedroom, and we began our practice of becoming invisible. My mother changed her shopping habits, now buying our groceries, meat, and vegetables at varying stores so local neighborhood merchants would not notice that a customer they knew had ration cards for three people rather than the two she'd had before. Every few weeks, she and I would also take a long walk through one of the narrow streets across a bridge to the other side of the canal where, in a small tobacco store, we met Mr. V, who was in charge of keeping hidden people fed and clothed. He supplied my mother with the fake ration cards that would be needed to feed an extra mouth, especially since food rations were becoming scarcer.

Nel brought a new richness to our little household. Shrouded in secrecy, as she needed to be in our dangerous, Nazi-occupied world,

I was not to know her last name, nor was I ever told her exact age. Young enough to be called a "girl" by both Mr. V and Mr. Sleumer, but old enough to be called a "woman" by my mother, she simply became an older sister to me, sometimes seeming closer in age to my mother but at other times closer to mine.

We quickly developed an almost sibling-like playfulness that at times got us into trouble with my mother. One morning as I left for school, I asked her to stick her hand through the curtains of the front window and wave goodbye, which she playfully did as I waved back to her from the street. When my mother discovered our game, she dragged us both into chairs and lectured us on the "stupidity and thoughtlessness of a game that could get us all killed."

Nel agreed that my mother was right and we should both be contrite, but prejudice is a learned attitude, and it still continued to puzzle me. I simply could not comprehend why Nel could not show her face through the windows or outside our home, or why the Germans hated her so much and wanted to kill her just because she was Jewish. Since my mother always told me to trust God, I asked her why God would allow this.

My mother said in her usual no-nonsense way, "It is people, not God, who do this to each other."

At that time she brought out a large, thick Old Testament Bible with full-page illustrations of the Exodus stories. The book had been in her family since she was a little girl, and her father had read the biblical stories out loud as she and her nine older siblings sat around the dinner table in their large childhood home in Rotterdam. Now in the evenings, the three of us—Nel, my mother, and I—sat around our small dinner table and explored the stories together. I especially liked the stories of God helping the Hebrews escape from slavery in Egypt, and I was mesmerized by the illustration of Moses parting the waters and then closing them up again after his people had crossed. It reassured me that if God could create miracles and free Nel's people from those cruel Egyptians way back then, surely He would save them from the cruel Germans now.

The sepia pictures in the old Bible included images of women dancing and playing their tambourines or timbrels in celebration of their freedom. It was either Nel or my mother—I forget which—who taught me that one of the women was Moses's sister Miriam, a powerful prophetess. But I remember the three of us dancing around the table clanging our spoons to celebrate "freedom," until my mother had to "shush" us because we could not risk the neighbors hearing us and becoming suspicious.

"What is a prophetess?" I of course wanted to know, and they explained that a prophet knew things other people didn't, often things that would not happen till way in the future. I told Nel that my mother and grandmother, with their ability to understand dreams and foretell the future, must be prophetesses, and she agreed with me that was a good thing indeed.

As an only child who had envied friends and cousins with brothers and sisters, I found Nel, in fact, an answer to my childish prayers. Everything about her fascinated me. I loved her beautiful, thick dark hair, and the fact that she wore glasses and shared with me that she "couldn't see a thing without them" convinced me that she must be very intelligent. In the way I imagined a sister would, she showed an interest in everything I was learning, reading, or had to say. I knew to keep silent about her presence to friends at school and in the neighborhood, but found myself rushing home to see her after classes were over. She was mine, and I was the happiest girl alive when she began to call me her "little stepsister" and gave me the affectionate nickname of "Hennepiet."

From the start, it was agreed that I would sleep with my mother so Nel could have her own room, but it did not take long for Nel and me to curl up together like sisters and fall asleep in each other's arms, and soon we were regularly sleeping together in my bed, a wide, double Murphy bed that folded up against the wall during the day.

Like a true older sister, she wrote a verse filled with love and wise counsel in my little friendship book. Dated June 1944 and written in Dutch in her strong and graceful handwriting, it told me (translation mine):

*Sweet Henny.*
*When perchance in later years,*
*you look in this album*
*and you read this verse.*
*Remember always the time*
*that we were together.*
*That you lay in my arms*
*and could keep me warm.*
*Dear sweet little girl, I too*
*will think about the happiness*
*we shared.*
*Your foster sister, Nel*

I had to accept that I was not to ask Nel any questions or tell anyone about her. But from the biblical stories my mother shared with us, it seemed to me that people had been doing horrible things to each other forever and ever. I asked her why people couldn't learn to be kinder to each other.

"People are still learning," she said. "The stories are God's way of teaching us the difference between good and evil and remind us that He is here to help us. But you must pray to Him."

And so I prayed to God that he would use his miracles to keep us all safe: Nel, my mommy, my daddy, my oma, my uncle Dick, and my cousins Netty and Loura, and, "Please, please use your miracles to make every one learn to be kind."

This was before I reached the age when I would decide that the miraculous lay not so much in the sweeping events of the biblical tales as in the love and courage of the hearts and sovereign spirits of these two women that I loved, my mother and Nel. They held me close and made me feel safe, even though they knew that heartless cruelty and the threat of cold-blooded slaughter lurked just outside the door of our home.

## Chapter 10

# Friend or Enemy?

As the war moved toward its fifth year in 1944, and the hope of a speedy victory and rescue by the Allies diminished, nerves were getting frayed and fears heightened among the people in the center of our old city. Friend and foe became more difficult to identify. Houses were being searched on the slightest pretense in the Nazi hope of finding a Jewish family to eliminate, an able-bodied Dutchman to use as slave labor, or an underground lawbreaker with a printing press or a radio transmitter to be shot in a public display of brutal Nazi power. The German Gestapo and Dutch Nazi collaborators' lust for bullying and raiding seemed to have no limits, and most residents sought safety in quiet invisibility within the walls of their homes.

All resources had dwindled and my mother and I had to deal with my rapidly growing body and the lack of available clothing. She now unraveled my old, outgrown sweaters and, with Nel and me seated next to her with our forearms outstretched, she wound the crinkly old wool around our wrists to create the skeins of yarn that would be used to knit a new, larger sweater out of my two old ones.

The months went by quietly, almost uneventfully. We got up in the mornings, I attended school; we went to bed at night and ate, drank, laughed, and cried in the times between as any normal family might. We were a gentle little household where reading to each other was a favorite pastime. The soft sounds of Nel and my mother's conversations that drifted leisurely on the aroma from their endless cups of coffee permeated our home with a temporary sense of well-being and female warmth and nurturing. Nel made plans for her future after the war, when she would be able to walk safely outside and make a life for herself once again, and my mother and I waited and planned for my father's return.

After Nel had moved in with us, Mr. Sleumer also became a more regular visitor to our home, bringing news of the war and the resistance as well as the occasional new stamp for my album and even a cigar band or two that my collection still lacked. He shared his stories with my mother and Nel, and when I was tucked in bed, they listened to the broadcasts by Radio Orange on one of the two illegal radio receivers. The whispers of their adult voices that reached softly across the hallway to my bedroom, where I lay curled up under the blankets, were to me the sounds of reassurance that we were on the right side of things in a dangerous world.

And on some of the mornings after Mr. Sleumer had visited, my mother took her usual stroll through the long narrow street of the black marketers, and across the bridge to the other side of the neighborhood for a chat with Mr. V. She had always displayed a good mind and memory for numbers and addresses and never wrote anything down. Once in a while I got to accompany her.

Schoolchildren of my age did not spend much time in each other's homes then. We did not have "playdates" in those days, and what with people hiding and soldiers raiding, my favorite place was to be at home with Nel and my mother. But I did happen to find myself at a classmate's home one afternoon. She had been sick, and her mother thought it was a good idea to have a couple of schoolchildren over to cheer her up. I guess you could call that a kind of a "playdate." Her name was Sonja, and when my mother dropped me off at her grand home on the Prinsengracht, one of the canals close to our home, Sonja's mother answered the door. She thanked my mom for letting me visit, took me by the hand, and led me into a black-and-white tiled entry hall that was bigger than our entire living room.

I noticed right away that Sonja's mother was very pretty with blond-reddish hair that curled over her shoulders. Her hands felt soft and she smelled of roses, which I guessed must be her perfume. She wore a shiny, pale blue blouse that was clasped at her neck by a large golden pin that looked like angel wings or maybe a butterfly; I wasn't sure which, and I knew it would be rude to stare.

She took me upstairs to Sonja's room, where our other classmate already sat on the floor next to the largest dollhouse I had ever seen even in pictures. It had four floors and furniture that looked like regular furniture, only much smaller of course. It even had little dolls that looked like actual people. I thought Sonja was very lucky to live in such a beautiful large home and have this big dollhouse. The three of us took turns being Mommy and Daddy to the children in the doll family and had fun rearranging the tiny furniture.

The time went by quickly, and after a while, Sonja's mother came up to tell us she was serving cups of hot cocoa in the living room downstairs. The cocoa tasted warm and sweet, and Sonja's mother joined us as we sat like grown-ups in deep cushioned chairs where she engaged us in conversation. I decided I really liked Sonja's mother. And in answer to her friendly questions, I told her, "No," I had no brothers or sisters. I did not tell her about my stepsister Nel, of course, because Nel was my big secret, but I did tell her that my dad was in a camp in Germany and said proudly, "He is a prisoner of war," because I did not want her to feel sorry for me.

"Oh, that must be lonely for you and your mother," she said in a kind, soft voice that sounded like she understood.

Then it was time to go home.

"Wait, come with me," she said, motioning me to follow her to the kitchen where she handed me a small bag with two cookies. "One for your mom, one for you."

I wished I could have asked her to give me one for Nel also, but, of course, I couldn't do that.

And that's when I saw the mugs on the kitchen counter. Mugs with swastikas painted on them. Swastikas! The sign of the hateful Nazis! The sign of the enemy that was plastered all over our city of Amsterdam to show that they were our bosses! Even our teacher at school had talked about the sign of the swastika. I glanced again. Yes, there they stood on the counter, swastika mugs!

For a moment I could not breathe. I did not dare look up at Sonja's mom, and my hands trembled as I took the bag of cookies out of her hands, her soft hands. And I don't remember exactly how I made it to the door where my mother was waiting for me.

"Did you have a nice time?" my mother asked, taking the bag of cookies out of my hand. "Did you thank Sonja's mother?" Then, "What's wrong?"

"They are bad people," I replied, and grabbing her hand tight, I told her about the mugs with swastikas painted on them.

"Oh, God." My mother sighed. "They are everywhere."

"How could she be so nice?" I asked.

"Sometimes people are just ignorant, just plain ignorant," my mother replied.

"She's still a bad person," I said and reassured my mother that I had not told her about Nel.

My mother explained that it would be best not to talk with anyone about what I had seen. She shook her head and frowned. "You are so young to have to understand how easily people can be misled and go wrong."

After that I did not visit Sonja's home again. Funny thing was that she and I never talked about it when we continued to see each other daily at school. We all had our secrets. It was just the way of our world. One day, when we were much older, we would be called the "silent generation."

I began to understand why my mother repeated so often that it was important no one be invited into our home, even people we thought we could trust, and her rule that if there came an unexpected visitor, Nel was to hide in my mother's bedroom immediately. No one, absolutely no one, could be trusted with our secret.

There were times, though, when it seemed it might be impossible to hide Nel's presence from the neighbors with whom we lived, one family on top of the other, in our urban beehive apartment complex. Six apartments, three on each side, with four doors opening onto the central portico from which the steps we all shared led down to the street. As on the warm afternoon when I caught one of the neighborhood boys on his knees outside our front door trying to look through the wide mail slot into the hallway of our apartment.

His sister and I were friends, even though we attended different schools, and I had told her I did not like her brother very much because he often teased me.

"Oh," she had said, laughing, "he just teases you because he likes you a lot," which I thought was just weird and a little creepy.

"My mother says you are hiding someone," he challenged me that day when I caught him looking into the mail slot.

"We are not," I yelled, but could feel my face blush hot and red.

"My aunt heard you all talking and laughing," he taunted me.

"You don't even have an aunt," I retorted, although I was not at all sure about that, but I knew that his sister had never mentioned having an aunt before.

"Oh, yes, I do," he said, smirking, and added, "She heard you through the open windows, and she has friends who can get you into trouble. Big trouble!"

I told him he was a liar and, slamming the door behind me, I ran inside and told my mother about the conversation. She looked more worried than I had expected. I thought she trusted our neighbors, but she reminded me that even though our neighbors were good people, we did not know our neighbors' relatives or friends, and these were unpredictable times.

She and Nel agreed that we all needed to be more careful. They made a rule that we should always remember to keep our voices down when talking with one another, especially when the windows were open. We had to make extra certain that the door between the front hall and the rest of the apartment was always closed, so no one could look through the mail slot and see Nel when she walked from the bedroom to the bathroom and the rest of our home. My mother also decided that Nel should not turn on the faucets in the kitchen, flush the toilet, or make any noise when my mother and I were not at home.

We resumed our domestic rhythm in the weeks that followed, and we found our way back to our hopeful selves and stories for the future. But our home did not feel as safe as it had before. The enemy had stuck his foot in the door, and he no longer just looked like a German soldier.

# Chapter 11
# The Betrayal

L ate one night toward the end of that chimerical summer, a loud banging on the front door permanently disrupted the illusory safety of our carefully guarded domestic tranquility.

I had been in a deep sleep when I was jolted awake to the repetitive sound of heavy fists pounding on the front door. Harsh, angry male voices yelled, "Open up, open up, open up now!"

Shaken and confused, I sat upright and looked around in my bed. The space next to me where Nel had lain asleep was empty.

The fists hammered on the door even louder as the thundering voices boomed their insistent, "Open up now, open up!"

Rubbing the sleep out of my eyes, I stumbled into my mother's adjoining bedroom, where I saw my mother on her knees on the floor trying to help Nel slide her body under the double bed that stood in the corner of the room.

"Hide, hide, go scrunch in the far corner," she urged Nel as she thrust her a bedspread to use as a cover.

When we did not open the front door in response to their loud insistent commands, the voices outside suddenly became muffled.

We heard them talking to each other, then sounds of shuffling, more shuffling, and then . . . nothing. Quiet. Silence. My mother held my hand as we breathed a momentary sigh of relief. Had they left? I felt the *thump, thump* of my own heart. Suspense in the face of tyranny differs from the suspense found in entertainment; it is real, and the body remembers it even years later. I took a deep breath, but it hurt my chest, and I pushed myself closer to my mother. Then, a heavy splintering noise, sounds of ripping wood and shattering glass.

"Oh, God," my mother whispered.

I heard the back door with its glass windowpanes leading into the kitchen being kicked in. Heavy footsteps crunched on broken glass. Before I could take another breath, three large men in heavy boots stomped through the living room and hallway into my mother's bedroom where, with a sardonic laugh, they immediately searched the closet and looked under the bed. I watched as they dragged Nel out by her feet. One of the men held a revolver in his hand. He ignored me but used it to push Nel and my mom into the dining area of our living room. One of the other men dragged two upright dining room chairs away from the table and placed them back to back. He ordered my mother and Nel to "sit down" facing away from each other.

I walked over to my mother, but the man without the gun told me to sit down on another chair in the living room and ordered me to "be quiet." When he addressed me in Dutch, I realized suddenly that he was not a German, but a betrayer, one of the hated Dutch Nazis who believed in Hitler's Third Reich of "superior people" that I had already learned more than enough about in my short life.

How does the presence of predatory hatred and cruelty impact a child? It would be a long time before I could access any emotions that I might have experienced in the traumatic hours that followed, but I would always be able to play back the images and sounds. It was as if I internalized the brutal events of that night as a movie or a play that I could watch and witness and even record on my memory screen, but in which I did not have an emotional part.

I watched for a long, long time as the men stood over my mother and Nel. Their loud, threatening voices bullied and interrogated each of them with harsh, rapid repetitions of questions that echoed in my ears like staccato gunfire. Then, after many hours, one of the men walked Nel out our front door. I watched her being led away by him. I think I wanted to run after her, but I could not move. Did she look back at me? Maybe she did or maybe she did not. I would only be able to recall her being led away, an image on a memory screen, an image like that of the little girl who had been led away to the green truck. Such a long time ago; when I was still able to walk with my daddy and I believed everyone was free and there was no need to hide. Maybe I could not move or feel because I was too busy watching the man with the revolver in his hand shove my mother to another chair at the dining room table, where he stood over her and laughed a cruel, harsh laugh. Frozen in place, I could only observe and be very, very still.

He asked my mother a question about others she knew in the resistance movement, and I pictured the friendly face of Mr. V in the tobacco store. I thought of Mr. Sleumer who listened to Radio Orange with my mother on the illegal radio receivers that were stored in the kitchen cupboard and the bedroom closet. I watched as my mom kept shaking her head and shrugging her shoulders.

Wanting to be closer to her, I slowly started to get up from my chair, but the man with the pistol turned around and barked, "Sit!"

I looked him over as I climbed back on my chair. I wanted to say, "You are a betrayer," and I wondered in silence why he did not look any different from other men. "A betrayer is the lowest of the low, even lower than the German Nazis themselves," my mother had told me.

A suffocating stillness had engulfed the room. It obliterated all sound, but for some odd reason my hearing seemed to sharpen. My mom looked at me from across the room, then at the heavyset Dutch Nazi standing over her holding his pistol.

"What will happen to my child?" she asked in a soft voice, nodding her head toward me.

I heard his snort as he laughed and said something to the effect of, "You should have thought of her before you took pity on that Jewess. She won't be your worry anymore. We'll know what to do with her."

My mother glanced at me and mouthed the words, *Pray, Henny, Pray.*

He expelled a brutish laugh, looked at his watch, and told her, "I am counting to ten. Maybe you will come to your senses."

As he began to count, I closed my eyes very tight and went deep into the silent place inside myself where there was only stillness, and there I asked the God of Nel and the God of my mother, that God who wanted those people in Egypt long ago to be free to *please, please, please help us.*

The counts came slow and measured: "One . . . two . . . three . . . ," but the numbers receded further and further until I could hear nothing. A terrible dark presence swirled around the room and began to suck me into its blackness. I could not breathe.

Then from across a large deep chasm, words pierced the dense air, softly uttered words, words in my mother's voice: "I am so sorry, but I have no names to give you. I guess you will have to take us away." With those words my mother sealed our fate.

"So." Like a bayonet, the harsh male voice with its sharp metallic edge now penetrated the thick darkness that had surrounded me. "You maintain that you have no contacts in the resistance, and I suppose you have no radio receiver hidden anywhere either."

Through the fog that shrouded my vision, I saw my mother shrug her shoulders and shake her head.

He gestured to his companion, who began to search closets, cabinets, and cupboards in the living room and finally the kitchen.

Strange as it may seem, through all this I watched with absolute attention. I observed, and I felt myself held in a deep stillness as the Dutch collaborator knelt down and methodically opened each kitchen cabinet. He took out all the pots and pans and then the china one piece at a time, leaving them strewn on the kitchen floor when he was finished. Finally he reached the cabinet with the fake wooden backing behind which one of the radios was hidden.

I would never be able to explain what happened after that. Why did I not feel afraid? Or did I but simply did not remember it? How do we store trauma? Probably I stopped breathing, and my psychological training would many years later suggest that I had dissociated, but at the time I could feel my mother praying across the room, and I matched myself to that faith and energy with every fiber in my young body. I aligned myself with something larger, the way I had once done when on my walks with my dad, I had matched my small steps, footstep by footstep, to his larger ones.

For the rest of my life, I would carry the visceral memory of that experience in the core of my being and assert without a doubt that the room filled up with a palpable flow of invisible dense energy that I could only describe in later years as a force field in motion. It was as if the air in the room had rearranged itself, and physical space, as we know it, ceased to exist.

I observed the Dutch Nazi collaborator take out the kitchen objects that stood in front of the fake partition: a small glass coffee grinder, a set of mixing bowls, a milk jug, several glasses, vases, and empty jars. He removed each object slowly and deliberately as if in slow motion and in a final act ran his hand across the fake back wall of the now empty cabinet. He stood up, gestured to his companion, and said in a dull tone, "Nothing."

His companion stared at my mother and pointing up to the pile of blankets and covers above the bedroom closet where the other radio was stored, asked: "How about the bedroom closets?"

My mother shrugged: "Go ahead, it's mostly stuff that belongs to my husband who is a POW in Germany. I don't even know if he is alive anymore."

"We'll make sure he is not," the man replied with another brutish laugh that landed his spit on my mother's face as he got up from the table to get something from the pocket of his jacket that lay on the floor.

The morning light had begun to filter through the living room windows, and it appeared he had decided it was time for him and his companion to have their breakfast. The lack of sleep made it difficult for me to keep my eyes open and remain seated on the upright chair I had been sitting on all night. Their ham sandwiches were large and smelled delicious. With the friendliness of a cat feeding a mouse, they offered my mom a piece. She refused but said they could give me some. I was allowed to sit on a chair next to her, but I could not eat. My stomach had a lid on it that could not be opened.

She took my hand and whispered, "Eat, it's all right."

I took a small bite of the sandwich segment that one of the men put in front of me, but I could not swallow it. I gagged and, retching uncontrollably, I ran to the toilet to cough it up.

This drew the men's laughter and sarcastic comments addressed to my mother about "stupid people who are raising their children to be weak." They finally finished eating their sandwiches and stood up from their chairs.

They were ready to leave and were not going to take us with them. "Not this time," the man with the pistol said. "Not this time, not yet."

My mother guessed that our apartment would be under surveillance. Right now she was the bait, the small fish with which they hoped to catch bigger fish in the resistance movement.

As they walked out the front door, they told her that it was "only a matter of time."

I held her left hand as she pointed with her right hand to a framed tile that hung in the hallway leading to the front door. It showed the Dutch flag waving in the wind on a bent flagpole. Underneath, the caption read, "Bent but not broken." The motto could have equally applied to my mother.

Her defiant gesture and words were met with scornful laughter. "We are not done with you yet." And with a final "Don't expect to see your husband alive again," the men stomped out the front door and slammed it behind them.

She took me in her arms. "Let's go to bed," she said. "Don't worry, God will take care of us."

I nodded. Had I not felt the air rearrange itself? "But, Nel?" I needed to know.

"We have to pray for her. She will come back. You will see."

And I believed her. Like Miriam in the old Exodus story of slavery and freedom, my mother was my prophetess. We curled up in her bed together, and I fell asleep immediately in her arms. The memories would not return to haunt me for many years, and then the feelings that were numbed and buried would spill out also, but by then I would be older than my mother was now.

# Chapter 12

# The Morning After

In the morning I awoke to find the side of the bed where my mother had slept empty. "Mommy?" I called out as I stumbled unto the floor and walked into the other bedroom that Nel and I shared for so many months. There was no one there. The image of a fat Dutchman leading Nel out through our front door flashed in front of my eyes. Did I have a bad dream?

"Mommy? Mommy?" Why was I shaking so? I put on my slippers and walked in my flannel pajamas through the hallway into the living and dining room. "Mommy?" My voice echoed off the walls of the empty rooms. No smell of the coffee that she and Nel always made in the mornings. No sounds of their voices in conversation. Where was my mother? Where was she? I took a step into the kitchen where cool morning air struck my face because the splintered door onto the back verandah still stood wide open. My heart thumped too fast, and I could not breathe very well as I stepped carefully over the broken glass that still covered the floor, visible remnants of the night's invasion and horror.

It had not been a dream. But where was my mother? Did the Nazis come back and take her too? I called out again, louder this time, "Mommy! Mommy!" My voice pleaded for her to answer.

That's when the inhuman noises reached my ears. The sounds seemed to rise up from the bottom of the wooden stairs that led from the back verandah down into our small urban yard space. Surrounded by high red brick walls that divided the narrow building lots in the old city, there was not much down there except for a few square meters of barren dirt and the shed in which my dad stored his tools. What could those hideous noises be? I stepped carefully across the threshold of the splintered door onto the back verandah. My heart did its weird *thump, thump* again, and my chest hurt. I choked as I tried to swallow back tears. Perhaps I should go back inside and wait for my mother? But as if possessed, I kept shuffling my feet toward the awful sounds.

Was someone being killed? I never knew what motivation kept propelling me forward, except that I desperately wanted my mommy. The noises grew more distinct. A chilling mixture of anguished moaning and splintering sounds rose up like the cries of a small animal in the throes of slaughter, its skull and bones being hacked and broken. Then I heard her sobs.

"Mommy? Mommy?" Shaking, barely able to breathe, I ran out onto the verandah. At the top of the wooden steps, I looked down and saw the top of her head below me. Her hair wild and unkempt, she was on her knees bent over the barren dirt ground. She was holding a hammer high above her head and bringing it down with a violent cry, over and over and over again as if she were holding a weapon. I could hear her sobs and mutterings over the crashing splintering noises as she smashed to bits the radios that had given us the comforting sounds of Radio Orange. Pieces of wood and metal flew all around her head with each stroke of the hammer. There was a spade next to her, and I saw holes in the hard ground where she had dug small graves for the radios that had been our link with my father and the good people who gave us hope.

When she lifted her head to glance up at me, I froze in place. Her eyes gleamed with an alien, unfocused darkness, a madness that did not see me but something evil. This woman at the bottom of the stairs was not my mother, not the mother I depended on with every part of my small being. This was a crazy, frightening woman whose eyes blazed with a wild terrible look of something I did not want to approach. How could this be my heroic strong mother on whom I could always lean?

Where was the woman I had trusted, the prophetess, the one who had told me that God would make everything all right? I wanted to run away from this crazy woman. Tears mixed with dirt streaked across her face, her tangled hair covered her forehead, her mouth twisted into something ugly. This was not the disciplined mother who comforted me, the mother who always imparted lots of information, even if I did not grasp it all. This was not the mother who had rational answers and solutions for everything that happened.

Then she called to me in a rambling tortured voice. "I have to get rid of these. They will be back, you know," she cried. "They will be back and they must not find these."

Her wild, demanding eyes buried into mine, and zombie-like I felt myself obey and proceed down the wooden steps where at the bottom, I knelt down next to her on the hard ground and began to help bury the bits and pieces of the remaining evidence of our resistance to tyranny and oppression. My hands obediently picked up piece after piece of the smashed radios and put them into the holes she had so carefully dug. My hands seemed guided by another mind that knew exactly what to do, a mind from which I felt at that moment completely disconnected. For the truth was that I was numb, and I could feel nothing, nothing at all. I had lost the mother in whom I had put all my trust.

Even years later, when I tried to recall any feelings, I would be struck by the mind's amazing power to block the experience of terror.

I could access my mother's look of fear, her terror, even her momentary madness, but not my own. It was as if in that critical moment, we were fused into one single act of survival, an act that demanded our complete engagement in burying the pieces of the radios. All that mattered was to hide the evidence. The only point was survival. Our individuality, our feelings were of no consequence. Not at that moment.

*We will do this*, her voice screamed inside both our minds, and we did.

Suddenly a figure appeared at the top of the stairs. "I just heard," Mr. Sleumer's calming voice reached down to us. He strode down the steps and took my mother in his arms. "Come with me." He reached one hand to mine and walked us to the familiar house where Mia's parents proceeded to put my mother to bed.

Silencing her protestations about "the radios . . . and Henny. . . ," he looked at her with a kind but serious look.

"It's all right. I will take care of it." He turned to me. "She's going to be fine. You can't tell anyone."

"I know, I know," I replied with a flash of anger.

"Good, you are a brave girl."

I would only see him a few more times after that. My mother would tell me that our apartment was now under Nazi surveillance, and all contact with any resistance workers had to be broken. I could not tell anyone anything about what had happened. It would be as if there never had been any radio transmitters. As if no Mr. V or Mr. Sleumer had ever existed, and worst of all, as if I'd never had a secret stepsister named Nel who lived in our home and slept in the same bed with me. We were just an ordinary mother and daughter, dealing with that thing we humans so lightly call war, a mother and child coping daily with humanity's capacity for hatred, prejudice, and violence as parents and their children have done throughout history and continue to do all over the world to this day.

We stayed with Mia's family for only one night. My mother recovered quickly, a fact that she credited not to her own strength but to the fact that she had me, a dependent, almost-seven-year-old child, to take care of. Mia's mom engaged me in supporting my mother, and that strategy in turn helped me be the "brave girl" I aspired to be. The following day we moved back to our empty apartment where once again it would be just the two of us, my mother and I.

For weeks after Nel was taken away, our activities and home were watched. Each day upon leaving for school or coming home, I witnessed the man in black shiny boots walk back and forth on our street; sometimes he leaned against the wall or slouched near our porch, but always he was watching, always watching. I could not say for sure if it was the same man all the time. I never looked at his face, only the black boots, but he may as well have been. His was the figure of the betrayer, the traitor, an archetype that would in later years appear in my dreams and nightmares as a skulking rat.

I missed Nel's young laughter and the way she could banter with my mom and fill our home with their combined voices of sweet hope. I missed the sounds of the radio in the evening when in my bed I had felt secure with the presence of Mr. Sleumer, my mother, and Nel in the living room just down the hall.

But I would soon learn that war does not permit the luxury of grieving or processing trauma. Those are gifts of peacetime. War demands total presence in the here and now. Memories needed to be locked away in order to access the raw energy necessary for survival. Other quite different challenges still lay ahead.

# Chapter 13

# Risk-Taking Mothers

S ome time after Nel was seized from our home and following
my seventh birthday in September of 1944, food rations in
Amsterdam were steadily reduced. The Allies lost a major battle
near the town of Arnhem in Southeast Netherlands that month and
were forced to leave the provinces of North and South Holland that
contained the cities of Amsterdam, Rotterdam, and The Hague in
the hands of the Germans. With food supplies dwindling and no
immediate hope of liberation, the housewives in our neighborhood
began to gather in the small portico of our apartment building and
in the street below to share their worries about survival with one
another.

"It looks like we are going to have a long cold winter," said "Aunt"
Riek, the mother of a little boy whose door opened onto the portico
across from ours.

"Yes, and the Allies have abandoned us," said the usually quiet
mother of five who lived nearby.

"They're more concerned with capturing Berlin than liberating us,"
my mother joined in.

"How are we going to feed our children if this war goes on any longer?" the mother of five asked.

The adults no longer bothered to hide the truth from us children. Young and old, we were now all in survival mode together, and lack of food became the main topic of conversation among the adults upon whom we children depended.

It seemed that all possible forces now combined to destroy us. Although American troops had liberated the southern tip of the Netherlands, the Allied Forces were focused on conquering Nazi Germany and not on freeing our occupied northwest corner of the Netherlands. Nature, we were told, was preparing to send Europe one of the coldest winters in recorded history. And the Nazis, in retaliation for a Dutch railroad strike, had blown up dikes and pumping stations and flooded large areas of the country that lay below sea level. Imprisoned by surrounding water, our small northwest corner of Holland became an isolated fortress where German troops and Dutch citizens together would face the rapid depletion of food and fuel supplies.

But while the food situation was already becoming desperate in the center of Amsterdam, the farmers beyond the city still had ample homegrown supplies. This started the phenomenon known as the "hunger trippers," hungry urbanites, men and women who in increasing numbers trekked out to the farms in the hope of being able to buy some eggs, cabbage, or potatoes to feed their families. In the absence of trains, buses, or automobiles, they rode their bicycles or even walked, some pushing empty baby carriages they hoped to fill with farm produce, far out into the countryside beyond Amsterdam. It could be an exhausting and hazardous journey of many kilometers, often in sleet and cold. Many of the roads were blocked by German troops, a kind of food Gestapo, whose job it was to stop the "hunger trippers" on their return and who often confiscated the supplies for their own use.

My mother still had a small supply of the dried red beans that had sustained us for a couple of months now, but soon we would have nothing except the meager rations that were being reduced weekly. Our neighbors pointed out that people on the streets in Amsterdam were already beginning to show signs of malnutrition, and my mother, always the planner, decided that she should make a trip on her bicycle out to the farmlands to see if she could get us a few pounds of extra potatoes.

"Potatoes store well," she told me, "and if we're careful, they can help carry us through the famine that is being predicted."

"If this one goes well, maybe I'll even make a few more trips," she added with renewed confidence. "I am not going to let us starve."

Since large numbers of city people were now hunger tripping, my mother assured me that she would not be in any real danger except possibly to come home empty-handed.

I felt more reassured, however, when she told me that her plan was to go with a neighbor who was an athletic woman my mother's age or perhaps a few years younger. She was the mother of the girl whose brother I did not like, especially after he had looked through our mailbox and made those awful threats, but he had not bothered me since then, and my mom had told me that it was not his fault that the Nazis had taken Nel.

"He is just a little boy," my mother had said. "I even suspect his father may be hiding so that he won't be sent to work in Germany."

And his sister told me that her brother was just an awful tease.

So I decided to ignore him.

The plan was for me to stay with Hedi's family that day, and when our mothers prepared for their joint bicycle journey into the country-side, Hedi and I took it as a sign that we were meant to be best friends. Her father had been too weak to work for a long time now. He did not have the strength to make the journey into the countryside, she told me, and her mother complained every day that the diminishing rations were not enough to sustain a sick man and two growing children. I thought that perhaps he was hiding as my mother had said, but I did not bother Hedi about that. Secrets were secrets.

On the morning of their departure, the sky hung low and heavy over a cold, wet autumn day. Hedi's mother and my mom would have to ride in the rain for several hours, and they had bundled up for the long trek ahead as they set off early on their bicycles. Hedi and I played together that whole day, pretending we were twins and waiting anxiously for our mothers to return. They had not arrived home by the time we expected they would. Darkness began to settle outside, and once again in the home of kind strangers, I fretted about losing a person close to me. As the time slipped away further into the evening and our mothers still had not returned, I did my best to push away the old familiar presence of fear, but it crept in behind my eyes, in my throat, in my chest, and even in my stomach where it made me feel nauseous. Hedi's brother as usual teased that we would all end up in an orphanage, but his father told him to be quiet and he ended up sulking in a corner of the room.

Hedi and I rolled our eyes, and she whispered, "He's such a spoiled baby," which made me feel better and like her even more.

Luckily, just a few minutes later, we heard sounds of laughter on the stairs and watched our two mothers, wet, bedraggled, and shivering with cold, walk in through the door carrying two sacks with a dozen or more large potatoes in each sack. The two women laughed and chattered with an exhilaration that sounded like they had come home with bags of gold nuggets instead of a few potatoes. Their experience had clearly created a bond of friendship between them, and we all spent the evening together as they shared the story of their adventure over hot tea.

The bicycle ride into the country had been cold and tiring but uneventful, Hedi's mother said, and the couple that owned the farm where they stopped was "friendly and really warm and supportive."

"Yes," my mother said, "they even fed us bread and coffee and sold us the potatoes at a very reasonable price," which apparently was not always the case.

The ride home was not so simple, they told us. A German patrol blocked the roadway and searched several bicycle riders ahead of them. My mother spotted the patrol from a distance, and they decided on a plan that might prevent the confiscation of their precious bags of potatoes. Hedi's mother had some acting experience and also had the advantage of being an attractive blonde, both mothers added with a giggle. Their plan, they told us, was that my mother would take both sacks of potatoes and hide them under her raincoat.

"If they looked at me too closely, I would just look fat or pregnant," my mother said with a laugh.

Hedi's mom would pretend to have an accident on her bicycle and create a distraction while my mother rode past the two Germans.

"It was a silly plan, and we had no idea if it would work," my mom said as they both giggled again like two schoolgirls, "but we were not about to give up our potatoes, so we had to give it a try."

My mother was a strong bicycle rider and could handle the two sacks of potatoes with ease, she said. She also was the faster rider of the two, so she stayed behind while Hedi's mom approached the German guards, faked a fall from her bicycle, cried out for help, and distracted the two young men long enough for my mother to ride past swiftly without being challenged. As they retold their story to us, they both roared with laughter at the "dumb German guards" who were apparently "not much more than boys and so easily seduced by a pretty blonde woman in distress." Encouraged by their success, they began to make plans for their next trip. However, the next time never happened.

The German troops themselves were in need of food now, and the blockades became stricter and more dangerous. The weather with temperatures below freezing had also become more threatening, and many of the farmers themselves were running low on supplies. They had to take care of their own families and were no longer so ready to look kindly upon the hungry urbanites demanding food. My mother decided that, despite our diminishing food supply, the trips to the farms had become too risky. She also admitted she was beginning to feel the effect of the restricted rations and was not as strong as she had been on that first trip, but for a little while we enjoyed the luxury of those extra potatoes that my mother rationed out carefully. Hedi and I became temporary "best friends" in the shared glow of being the daughters of heroic, risk-taking mothers who refused to let their families go hungry.

# Chapter 14
# The "Miracle" Moon

One evening in October as the weather grew colder, I watched my heroic mother march through our apartment, yanking chains and pushing buttons for ceiling lights and single lamps till every room in our home blazed with light. Perplexed, I followed her silently as she strode into our small kitchen where she struck a series of matches and lit every single jet on the gas stove, including the oven. With all the gas jets alight and burning at full power, she placed two straight-backed chairs in front of the gas stove, opened the oven door, and ordered me to sit.

I obediently climbed on one of the chairs but was almost knocked backward by the intense blast of heat from the open oven and flame-shooting gas jets that beat against my face and chest.

"I want you to feel this warmth and see all the light and always remember it," my mother said as she sat down next to me, her eyes locked onto mine, her cheeks reddened from the heat. "We are facing cold, dark days, but I want you never to forget this feeling of warmth and light, and I want you to know that no matter what happens, all this light and warmth will return."

I nodded, not at all sure I understood what was going on, but I told her that I would remember. And indeed, in my adult years when unavoidable dark or challenging times, to which none of us is immune in this life, dimmed my joy and pulled me into hopelessness, I would picture the lit-up apartment, see my mother's reddened cheeks, feel the flames of heat on my body, and remember her message that "the warmth and light will return."

My mother and I went to bed warm that night but awoke the next morning to a bitterly cold apartment shrouded in winter darkness, the electric power and gas having been turned off indefinitely in the city of Amsterdam. We were blessedly still spared the knowledge that we were about to face one of the coldest winters in history and that within the next five months some twenty thousand of our fellow citizens would die of cold and starvation.

By Christmas our once-beautiful city of Amsterdam had already entered into a death spiral. Canals were freezing over, and most food supplies had disappeared from the stores. Transportation had vanished from the streets with the exception of bicycles, and here and there a cart pulled by a malnourished horse or by an old man ready to collapse. Garbage had begun to pile up on the streets and in the canals. But inside our home, my mother insisted that I wash my face and brush my teeth, and that we make our beds every day.

"If we keep ourselves and the house clean, it means that we are still in charge and not giving up hope," she repeated daily.

And on Christmas morning, she surprised me with a box that contained a new rag doll with a china head, one of the last of the few available dolls in town for which she had stood in line outside the department store for hours in freezing temperatures. I named the doll Gretha after my aunt in Rotterdam, my mother's sister and the mother of my favorite cousins, Netty and Loura. The doll completed my symbolic extended family, a group of dolls named after my favorite family members over whom I presided with imaginary tea parties.

I served delicious make-believe pastries and enjoyed enlightened conversations complete with pronouncements I had picked up from my mom and made my own. Inside our home, love, imagination, and hope still survived, even as the city of Amsterdam became a cold, dark hollow where its inhabitants would slowly begin to grapple with the life-threatening impact of unheated homes, malnutrition, and hunger in freezing temperatures, with no sign of hope for a speedy liberation.

As the year crept toward its inevitable end and the bitter cold intensified, my mother joined the untold numbers of people in our city who felt the need to seek solace in the rituals of childhood religions that offered them the support of communal hope and prayers.

"On New Year's Eve we are going to church," she announced. "We need to pray for peace."

With the exception of my christening in the esteemed New Church on the Palace Square when I was two years old, an event of which I had no memory but of which my mother retained a treasured certificate, I had never been to church, and I felt excited at the prospect.

My mother had chosen a church where a minister known to her as a member of the resistance was leading the evening service.

"A good man," she told me.

The church lay several city blocks from our house, and frigid temperatures with blackout conditions on that New Year's Eve would necessitate our careful navigation of ice-covered bridges and slippery sidewalks. Heavy black clouds obscured the sky and shrouded our path in early darkness as, bundled up against the cold, my mother and I set out. It felt as if all the light that could have guided our way had been obliterated by the powers of evil that now claimed our city as their own. Darkened lampposts, their luminosity extinguished, mocked our helplessness, while not even a sliver of light escaped to come to our aid from the blackout-covered windows of the homes by which we walked with care. In addition to the fear that we might slip and break a leg or an ankle, there was the ever-present danger that in the darkness, we could take a misstep and tumble into one of the canals where the ice might be too thin to hold a falling body.

It had already become a common occurrence to hear screams in the middle of the night that, I was told by my mother, belonged to yet another "poor soul," a desperate man or woman who had fallen or jumped in to end their life in the stagnant murky waters underneath the thin ice.

As our eyes tried to distinguish shapes and obstacles, and our feet felt for non-slippery surfaces to walk on, my mother and I held on to each other with a tight grip. We slowly crossed the ice-covered bridges and, step by cautious step, made our pilgrimage to the New Year's Eve service.

You would think, since it was my first time in church, that I would remember the service, but I really could never recall anything more than an uncomfortable feeling of having to sit still on a cold, hard bench, a pew, squashed between bundled-up grown-ups who were holding small lit candles that made me cough. Perhaps what happened afterward took up all the memory space in my brain for that evening.

My mother would tell me later that when the minister's sermon lasted longer than she had anticipated, she became concerned about our long walk home in the dark and the need to be safely inside before the hour of the German curfew. Nightly curfew for all of Amsterdam's Dutch citizens was 7:00 p.m. or 8:00 p.m., depending on the Nazi mood, and anyone still on the street after that time risked being imprisoned or even shot to death.

All I personally remember was a sense of relief when, after the closing hymn had finally been sung and the minister had given us a blessing, all the candles were extinguished, and I felt myself propelled along with my mother in the congregation's slow shuffle toward the large exit doors at the back of the church. A cold hushed darkness had descended on the church hall and, finding myself chest high to the adults whose rough winter coats brushed against my face and obscured my view of the open doors, I hung on to my mother's hand with a tight grip.

Suddenly, as if divinely orchestrated, a symphonic wave of "Ah . . . aah . . . aah . . . ooh!" rippled through the crowd from the open doors in the rear to the front of the church hall where we had been seated. United in one emotion, the many voices merged and rose for a moment in a single spontaneous collective expression of awe and surprise. When my mother and I reached the open doors, and the adults around me dispersed, my eyes blinked in a rapid adjustment from darkness to a blazing, blinding light. In front of us, a white, snow-covered scene lay outlined in glittering daylight brilliance, while just above its icy surface, almost touching it, hung a gigantic full moon so close and so large that if I reached out I was sure I could almost put my fingertips on it.

"It's a miracle, a miracle!" the voices of the congregants around us exclaimed, smiles on their thin, tired faces as they walked off with renewed hope to their cold, dark homes.

My mom hugged me. "Look, it's a miracle, Henny, look! God is with us, and He will guide us home safely. It's a miracle!"

In later years, my mother often referred with passion to that magical full moon that lit the way for us on the slippery sidewalks along the canals and across the icy bridges to find our way safely home. For her that full moon would always symbolize a gift from God the Father, a true miracle. For me the experience opened another portal into the great mystery of the universe that would haunt my imagination and one day set me on my own quest for the Divine. It imbued me with a sense of the sacred that was not bound by our understanding of things but could materialize itself in any shape any time it wished, perhaps even a bright gigantic full moon breaking through a cloud-covered sky on New Year's Eve. But whether through my mother's religious lens or my own imagination, it made the harsh world feel a little safer to both of us. Despite their brutal attempts to extinguish the light, the tyrannical powers did not have the final word that evening.

We managed to arrive home before curfew, and after unlocking the door to our dark, frigid apartment, my mother announced that she had another surprise for us. A ration card had been issued some time before for a few ounces of flour, and my always-disciplined mother had saved the flour for this particular night. Even though we had no gas, no electricity or wood, we still had a handful of anthracite coal as well as a stack of old magazines that lay stored in the hall closet. In a small ceramic bowl, my mother proceeded to mix the flour with cold water into a thin pancake batter. She told me to bring her my four-inch toy frying pan that I used in the make-believe tea parties with my dolls and smeared the little pan with the remains of the cooking grease she had also saved for this last night of the year. Like a priestess engaged in a sacred ritual, she carefully placed pieces of the torn and crumpled pages from the magazines on the small pile of anthracite coal in our cold, dark fireplace. We sat down on the floor with our legs crossed. She took a single match and lit the tiny fire that soon generated enough heat to bake four small, lightly browned pancakes.

I breathed in the delicious smell as she set two of the warm golden cakes on each of the small plates we held in our laps. No organized religious ritual or five-course expensive dinner would ever in my life match the power of that tender moment in which we said our prayer of thanks for the New Year and the liberation that my mother insisted was near. Warming ourselves by the glowing embers of the dying fireplace, I leaned against her on the floor and savored each tiny bit of pancake, one little bite at a time, and with each small, delicious bite, I borrowed some of my mother's belief in the endurance of the warmth and the light and made it my own.

We were alive to face the year 1945.

# Chapter 15

# The Hunger Winter

In January of 1945 Amsterdam was in the grips of the Hunger Winter with its horrific challenges of prolonged malnutrition and hunger, and the realization that many would die of starvation if we were not liberated soon. While the large world powers continued to fight the global battles for freedom, our personal lives shrank to survival level. At night the droning sounds of the Allied bombers heading for Berlin over our house reminded us that the fight for liberation continued, but for my mother and me, our neighbors, and the kids I went to school with, liberation had become a fantasy, a story in our imagination. We could only focus on the minutiae of staying alive.

I would wonder in later years how memory selects the images it wants us to retain in times of trauma. The things I remembered most clearly from the terrible months of hunger that lay ahead of us were: the little orange pan that held two slices of bitter, gooey bread made from tulip bulbs, the faux "meatball" in the soup-kitchen slop, my too-tight shoes, and the black-and-white cat on the garden wall.

On the first day of that fateful year, my mother sat at our dining room table and wrote a poignant letter to her mother and my uncle

Dick, my mom's brother with whom my grandmother still lived and survived in Rotterdam. My mother missed her family, and I knew that she was concerned for their safety because of circulating rumors about widespread "razzias," or roundups, in Rotterdam. The infamous roundups and mass shootings of innocent people had increased in both Amsterdam and Rotterdam. Men and women were being picked up at random, lined up en masse in garbage dumps or against blank city walls, and shot to death—sometimes on suspicion of having been involved in the resistance, other times as blind retaliation and senseless acts of Nazi brutality against the Dutch people.

Decades into the future I would have a chance to reread my mother's new year's letter when my uncle's daughter, born after the war, kindly passed it on to me. Writing on my father's old company letterhead, one of the last available sheets of stationery in our home, my mother expressed her worries about the "razzias" and implored her brother to let her know if family and friends were safe. Her letter conveyed the heartbreaking mixture of despair and the willful hope that kept us alive. "With a daily ration of two slices of dry bread in the morning and a visit to the soup kitchen in the afternoon, the food situation is hopeless," she wrote, "but we won't let ourselves lose courage. We now have a whole new year in which we can say, perhaps this is the year the war ends."

But Amsterdam was now completely cut off from the surrounding farmlands and food supplies, and as the cold weather of the winter of 1944–45 intensified, food supplies were dwindling rapidly. The occupying Germans distributed what meager provisions were left among their own troops, who were now as much prisoners of the isolated city as its Dutch inhabitants. From January into February into March and finally into April, our daily food rations would go from five hundred calories to two hundred calories per person, and eventually to nothing at all. World War II for many of the people of Amsterdam had now been reduced to a personal battle. The outcome would be determined by our body's strength to survive the cold and starvation. Our homes had become ice chests. Everything that was burnable in our freezing city became a source for survival: the trees along the canals, wooden park benches, the wooden blocks between the tramlines, and even doors, window frames, and wooden stairs of homes. Inhabitants of upstairs apartments were at risk of being trapped on the upper floors of their buildings. It was not uncommon to hear them scream at the desperate scavengers who were sawing or hacking away at the wooden stairways that led up from the street below. Food and warmth were all that mattered.

Bundled up in heavy winter clothes, I now slept permanently with my mother in her bed. On many mornings, I awakened to find the lace curtains stuck to the ice that had coated the inside of our bedroom windows overnight. I liked to pull away the curtain and trace the crystallized patterns with my fingers. My mother warned me that I was putting holes in the curtains, but something about the eerie beauty of the icy shapes and forms fascinated me. Beauty was hard to find that winter. War and hunger have a way of destroying beauty, but the human soul, for some reason, continues to remember and long for it.

The relentless cold and lack of food left us both weakened. My mother prayed a lot and, to stay warm, we curled up together fully clothed under the blankets, where we made up stories to entertain each other. Our stories mostly included delicious things to smell and eat. We imagined crusty hot bread smothered in butter, and my mom's meatballs in hot juicy gravy, and crisp fresh apples to bite into, and then chunky bars of chocolate. Of course, in our stories we always found a way to heat our ice-cold water for my mom's tea and my hot chocolate. To conserve our energy, we went to bed with the sunset and we didn't get up until late in the morning. Breakfast consisted of a ration of one slice of bread each. In years to come, I would vaguely remember the bread tasting like glue or wallpaper paste, but my mother corrected me and said it was made out of sugar beets until there were no more, and even more horrible-tasting tulip bulbs were substituted in the final months of the war.

We slept fitfully. Sometimes the steady drone of the Allied bombers flying back and forth over our roofs each night lulled me into a troubled sleep with violent scenes in which bombs were being dropped on Amsterdam instead of Berlin, where my mother said they were headed.

"They are friendly planes," she told me. "You can't sleep because you are hungry. Try not to think about it."

But my sleeplessness continued to worsen. I told my mother that my head would not let me stop thinking. If I fell asleep, there would be nothing to eat when I woke up, so I had to stay awake.

That's when she developed the daily ritual that eased my anxiety. Before we went to bed in the evening, she placed a small covered orange-colored saucepan on the chest of drawers right next to the bed. In it she had put our daily ration of two slices, one slice each, of the gooey substance that was supposed to resemble bread. We slept as late as our bodies would let us, and before I got up to wash my face and change my clothes, I brought the orange saucepan with the two precious slices into our bed with us. The kitchen cupboards having been completely emptied, it was, on most days, the only food available in our home. Huddled together, my mom and I said our prayers of thanks for our food and proceeded to take careful, small bites while we played a game of make-believe and pretended we were eating fresh hot bread with melting butter and a jam made of plump, juicy strawberries. Sometimes it worked.

Other times my mom's eyes filled with tears and she whispered, "It tastes like glue. I am so sorry."

I didn't know how to respond, so I just said, "It's good, Mommy."

In truth the empty, gnawing place inside me had no words. Even when I tried to remember it in future years, I could only access a hollowed-out feeling that attracted panic like a magnet. But the knowledge that the slice of bread, even if it was made from bitter tulip bulbs, sat within arm's reach next to the bed and would be there when I woke up in the morning helped me fall asleep in my mother's arms. Sometimes when I woke up during the night, and my head started to worry, I looked at that orange-colored pan and felt assured. There would be something to eat in the morning. And on rare occasions in my dreams, the gluey, sticky mess actually did transform into crusty bread with butter and jam, which had an odd settling effect on the gnawing pain in my belly.

Since I was a school-age child, I was also entitled to go to the soup kitchen for a daily lunch ration. Each school day, I joined the long line of other schoolchildren. We stood in line, armed with our personal little pots, pans, and pails, and waited patiently in freezing temperatures to receive a ladle full of thin, watery soup that we slurped down in the hope and promise that it might reduce the pangs of hunger.

One day I actually saw a roundish thing about an inch in diameter in the watery slush in my little pan, "A real meatball!" I said out loud.

It had been many months since I had eaten or even seen a meatball, but my mouth could still remember the taste of the ones my mother made, large and juicy, simmered in delicious gravy. They always made the house smell so good. I knew for certain that my mother had no lunch at all, so I ran the three city blocks home in my excitement to share my meatball with her.

"Oh, Henny, no, you should never leave the teacher and the other children," my mother admonished me, but she carefully sliced the round meatball into halves. We each put a small bite in our mouths, and both grimaced at the same time. It was a tulip bulb.

"It tastes awful," my mom said, "but eat it, it will keep you strong."

My second-grade class only met in the afternoons now. Fuel reserved for the schools had almost been depleted, and the furnace was only turned on for a few hours each day. We sat huddled close together in our seats, bundled up in coats and sweaters, a strange bunch of little children.

A few children looked better nourished. Some of the other children repeated what they overheard about them at home. "Their fathers probably sell stuff on the black market," or "Maybe their fathers work with the Nazis." Every so now and then a really thin little girl or boy whimpered with hunger and insisted, "We're all going to starve to death before the Allies liberate us," because that's what their parents had told them. But for the most part, we remained amazingly quiet about our experiences.

Lack of clothing and shoes became a big problem. We were seven- and eight-year-olds, and our bones were still growing, even though they no longer had much flesh on them. Many of us looked like little scarecrows with our spindly arms and legs sticking out of raggedy outgrown or oversized handed-down clothes. Little boys came to class in big brothers' outgrown jackets, and girls rated their mothers on their ability to sew their clothes and knit them sweaters. The best mothers were the ones who could transform curtains, sheets, and blankets into wearable pants, dresses, and jackets for growing children. We compared and even teased each other about our footwear. Some of the children, especially the boys, wore their parents' or other relatives' oversized shoes because they had outgrown their own. One of the boys, I remembered, had no shoes at all.

A teacher gave him a pair of her dead brother's shoes. They were too big, and our poor classmate stumbled when he first tried to walk in them. "Well, at least they will keep your feet from freezing," she told him.

When my toes began to push too hard into the leather front ends of my shoes, my mother carefully cut the front seam at the sole with a sharp knife so that my toes could have wiggle room, but she told me I had to wear thick socks and make sure I didn't stand in the cold too long.

"Yeah, you know what will happen if you do," two of the older boys told me when they saw the slit in my shoes. "Your toes will freeze, they will turn totally black, and then they'll fall off."

"Yeah," one of the boys added, "that happened to a cousin of mine, and then his foot, and then his whole leg turned black and had to be cut off."

Scared, I asked my mother, but she reassured me that I would not lose my toes or my feet or my legs and knitted me a pair of extra-warm socks out of the unraveled wool left over from one of the last old sweaters that I had outgrown.

I still liked school. It provided a few hours of reasonable warmth each day, and when my mind was occupied with the challenge of learning things, I forgot to feel hungry or scared for a little while. Arithmetic was one of my favorite subjects because numbers were predictable. I could make them fit together. I also loved to read. Words and sentences opened me to stories through which my imagination could wander afar in the way it did when my dad had told me fairy tales and mythic stories on his lap. Raised on the tales by the Brothers Grimm, I also made sure that in my stories good people always ended up happy and safe, and the bad people were punished severely.

I did not have a particular artistic talent, but I enjoyed drawing and liked to copy pictures of colorful flowers, ducks with ducklings, cats, and dogs—especially puppies. They reminded me that the world was once beautiful. When I looked at the pictures, I imagined that I would one day live in a house that had a garden with bushes that had large purple flowers, that I later learned were named rhododendrons. My garden would have beds of red and pink tulips and yellow daffodils, and of course that beautiful world of mine would include warm cuddly kittens and puppies.

I had not seen any live cats or dogs for a long time. Since the beginning of the Hunger Winter, all pets had disappeared off the streets of Amsterdam. Most had been eaten, either stolen and sold on the black market as rabbit meat, or sometimes put to sleep by loving owners who could no longer feed them.

One late afternoon, several weeks into the year, my mom and I were sitting bundled up in our chilly living room. We were hungry, cold, and bored. There would be no dinner that evening. No ration card had been issued that week, so except for a half loaf of tulip bulb bread that my mother had carefully portioned out to a slice each day, there was no food in the house. I asked my mother if we could eat some of the bread for dinner, but she explained that we had to make it last until the next ration card for another loaf of bread was issued.

"Henny, listen," she said. "If we eat a little each day, we will survive, but if we eat all the bread in one day and then have nothing the rest of the week, we will not." She taught me that survival depended on being disciplined.

It was near dusk. So, we decided we should just go to bed and try to sleep until we could eat our slice of bread in the morning.

That's when I saw him. With the shock of surprise, I stared through the glass of the French doors of the living room and pointed outside. "Mommy, mommy," I whispered. "Look!"

"Yes." She saw him too.

A skinny black-and-white cat rested on top of the brick garden wall that separated our lower level backyard from our neighbors. The wall adjoined my dad's toolshed, which he had covered with an extended corrugated iron roof that touched the deck of our back verandah. It would take only a few steps from the verandah, across the corrugated iron roof, to reach the top of that wall.

My mom moved swiftly. She slipped through the French doors onto the verandah without making a sound and crept across the deck.

"Here, kitty. Here, kitty," she called in the sweetest soft voice. "Here, kitty."

The cat remained motionless.

"Here, kitty."

He stared at her, but did not move.

My mother had reached the verandah railing. She would just need to climb over the railing onto the corrugated iron roof.

Then suddenly, as if he realized what she had in mind for him, that skinny black-and-white cat stood up and without a sound stole away along the top of the wall, down into our neighbor's backyard.

I let out the breath I had been holding without realizing, and sensed my relief. I knew in my bones that in my mother's eyes and maybe also in mine at that moment, that poor skinny cat had looked like food and not cuddly companionship.

"I've heard they taste like rabbit," my mother said softly when she walked back into the house. "But I couldn't have killed him anyway."

"And I would not have eaten him," I said, "but if he comes back, we could hide him."

My mother smiled. "Oh, honey, we don't have anything to feed him. But maybe he will catch himself a rat and survive."

"He'd better hide," I insisted, and my mother agreed, because that was the world we lived in. It was as if we were all in hiding now, human beings and pets alike, waiting for the Allies to liberate Amsterdam, waiting for the war to end. But many of us would die before then.

# Chapter 16

# City of Death

It had been almost two years now since my dad had left us, and in his absence our beautiful Amsterdam, the city with its stately seventeenth-century homes and tree-lined canals along which he loved to stroll, had become a dirty, treeless city that stank of death and decay. Emaciated old men, women, and children, some with distended bellies from hunger edema, struggled to last one more day, and perhaps another and another if they were lucky. Even though it was almost springtime, the brutal winter weather had not loosened its grip. To the east of Amsterdam, the Allied Forces had already liberated many cities, but our northwest corner of Holland lay abandoned and forgotten, imprisoned in the relentless Nazi grip of death.

On my way to school, I kept my eyes down and my woolen hat pulled down over my ears so I could not see or hear the overwhelming despair and ugliness of the death that surrounded me, but I was never able to escape the stench of it. My mother told me I had "a sensitive nose," but I did not know what to do about that, and she, who always had an answer for everything, offered me no solution. And honestly, the smells made me gag.

My daily track to school down the Prinsengracht took me past the sulfur heaters that had been placed alongside the canal to provide some modicum of relief for the people of Amsterdam, who were now dying at alarming rates from cold and starvation. The heaters that emitted a stench of rotten eggs were a gathering place for old men. At least in my mind they were old men. They were the leftover men, the men who were too old to be sent to work camps in Germany; too old, too sick, or in too deep a despair to bother to go into hiding or to be part of the resistance. Men who had been left behind, they were men of no use even to the cavernous appetite of war, bent over and diseased from hunger and freezing cold homes, disheveled in their old worn-out clothes, their bodies often unwashed due to lack of soap. Deprived of all hope and human dignity, many of them urinated out in the open, where the smell of their urine mixed with their stale body odors and the stench of rotten eggs that emanated from the sulfur heaters.

"Old men are disgusting," I told my mother one day after school, a comment to which she did not respond kindly.

"You need to feel sorry for them," she lectured me. "They are old and sick, and they are cold and hungry. The heaters give them a little relief from their suffering."

"Yes, but they don't have to pee in the street." I wrinkled my nose in judgment.

"Oh, Henny." My mother sighed. "They have lost the will to live. You are too young to understand. Try not to look at them or think about it," she urged.

So like the proverbial Three Wise Monkeys whose hands cover their eyes, ears, and mouth, I learned, along with many of the children in my school and neighborhood, to tune out the sights, sounds, and words of war's assault on human dignity. At least I tried hard to "see no evil, hear no evil, and speak no evil," but I'd be darned if I could avoid the smells.

Over time the kids I knew had all gotten used to the rolled barbed wire and the boot-stomping Germans with their loud "Sieg Heil" commands, their raucous marching songs and "Heil Hitler" greetings. We just pretended we didn't see or hear them. And we no longer paid attention to the splintering sounds of wooden stairs being ripped and pried out of homes by people desperate for wood to warm themselves. If we still heard the screams and curses from those who lived and would be trapped on upper levels, I wouldn't remember. We were even learning to avert our eyes and block our ears from the groans of the starving men and women collapsed on the sidewalks.

"They are dying," we said to each other, as if it were perfectly normal.

One day when a man walked by us with corpses piled up on a handcart, one of the older girls explained, "He's an undertaker. He takes the dead bodies away."

And an older boy said, "Yes, it's starvation, and my parents say that we will be next."

I asked my mother that day if she thought we were going to die of starvation also.

She said, "No, we are not."

She looked like some of the people I had seen on the streets, though. Her face showed dark hollows where she'd once had round pink cheeks, and her body no longer felt warm and soft. Now when she hugged me, I could feel her bones knock against mine.

"We'll be all right. God will help us," she assured me, and I made myself believe her.

But the next day when I walked down the front steps to go to school, I almost stumbled over an old man who lay slumped on his side against the wall of our house at the bottom of the steps. He was not moving, and I yelled up to my mother. Both she and a neighbor, whom the neighborhood kids called Aunt Riek even though she was not really our aunt, rushed out to see why I was yelling so.

They looked down at the man. "He's dead," my mom said and put her arms around me.

"Starvation," Aunt Riek whispered, "and we are next." She glanced at my mother and exclaimed, "Oh, Miep, he looks just like your husband."

I felt dizzy. This white-faced old man wrapped in a torn, dirty, old overcoat looked like my dad?

"No," my mother shook her head, "nothing like him."

"Come on." She took me by the hand. "I'll put on my coat and walk you to school."

She turned to our neighbor. "You'll take care of him?"

Aunt Riek nodded. "But you know they have run out of coffins."

"Yes," my mother replied, "I hear they are storing the bodies in one of the churches. The Old Church, I think."

On our walk to my school, my mother asked me how I was doing.

I said, "Fine," but needed to reassure myself. "That man did not really look like Daddy, did he?"

"Of course not." She looked at me surprised. "You see the photo of Daddy every day."

I didn't know how to respond. Memory has its unique way of living in our various senses. I always thought I would never forget my dad's face, but the man in the framed photograph that my mother sometimes kissed at night now seemed almost like a stranger. I did not kiss his picture, but sometimes I held his camera and thought I could feel his presence. My eyes did not hold his memory as strongly as the rest of my body, apparently. There were times when I could make myself be very still and go deep inside, and then I could almost feel the warmth of his strong arm around my back and shoulders and faintly remember his smell. The man who lived in that deep memory place made things with his hands—rubber straps to hold luggage on the back of a bicycle, a bookcase with glass doors to hold the many books he and my mother liked to read, and shelves for above my bed.

He smelled of rubber, wood, and paint, so different from my mother's citrusy scent of her favorite 4711 Eau de Cologne before she ran out of it.

But that had been a completely different world. Now no one smelled good anymore, not even of soap, which had disappeared along with everything else that was sweet-smelling. The city where he and I had walked to visit Uncles Jacob and Abe now stank of trash, of sulfur smells of rotten eggs, of urine and unwashed, dying old men.

Everything, absolutely everything, had changed since the ring of that doorbell when my dad was deported to Germany. His letters and photos had stopped coming a long time ago, but my mother still insisted that God would bring him back, and I made myself believe her. As long as I could still imagine the weight of his arm around my shoulder and remember his good smells, maybe he would, but sometimes I worried that he would be like the old men I saw on the streets.

When my mother dropped me off at school and explained to the teacher about my almost tripping over the dead man, some of the kids teased me for being late. Even in extreme times, little Dutch children of my era were taught to be punctual.

"You are in trouble," the boy behind me whispered in my ear as he pulled my hair.

I knew he liked me, but I didn't like him very much.

I had heard him boast to another boy, "My father doesn't think it would be so bad if Germany won the war."

The other boy had called him "a traitor," and the teacher had to pull them apart when they began to punch each other.

He pulled my hair again.

I turned around and said, "Stop it."

The teacher warned us to pay attention and proceeded with the class. We were just little school kids with the normal urge to laugh, tease, and play, but we were children of war immersed in an environment of deprivation, violence, and hatred. Most of us were feeling hungry, cold, and scared, and some carried big secrets that could not be talked about.

Some of my classmates lived in homes where subversive activities punishable by death were part of their everyday existence. In an effort to save human lives and undermine the enemy, their parents sheltered endangered human beings or used radio transmitters and printing presses to pass information. Other children went home to parents who arrogantly displayed the German swastika. Our life stories were being formed in the flesh and bone of our experience. But, whether the children of those who resisted the enemy or the children of collaborators and traitors, we would mostly remain silent as we wove the consequences of our parents' actions into the patterns of our own lives.

One day we would be named the "Silent Generation," a generation of kids born during the Great Depression and World War II. A demographic minority that was squeezed in between our heroic parents who fought for world freedom and earned the name of the "Greatest Generation," and the hordes of our younger siblings and our own children, the "Baby Boomers," who would set about to challenge and change the world as we knew it.

# Chapter 17

# The Inner World

I never could remember exactly when I began to have the recurring dream about the dark, swirling whirlpool—I guess you would call it a nightmare—or why I never told my mother about it. Perhaps because it started after I had accidentally left the front door open, and my mother's only winter coat and her bicycle, which she had hoped to exchange for food, were stolen from inside our hallway.

My mother and I had been seated in our living room when she told me that she was just going upstairs to ask a neighbor about a rumored ration coupon for bread.

"I'll only be gone a minute," she had said.

I amused myself with a jigsaw puzzle for a while but soon got bored and cold and wandered out the front door and up the stairs to the apartments above us to find her. I bumped into Maria. She and I were the same age, and I liked her, even though we did not have much in common. We attended different schools, and I was an only child living with my mother, while she was lucky enough to have both her mother and father at home as well as four siblings. Maria wanted to show me the large nativity scene that her mother had left displayed in their living room since Christmas.

It was unusual for her family to keep the nativity scene on display this many months after Christmas, she explained to me, "But my mother says that she will not put it away until the war ends."

She began to show me each of the figures around the crèche. Every figure was about the size of my pointing finger, except for the little baby in the crib that was much smaller, and I really liked the beautiful winged angel and the three wise men, who had seen the magic star in the sky. I wished we could have a nativity scene in our home, but when I once asked my mother, she had said that we did not do that because we were not Catholic. I didn't quite understand that since my mother also told me that we believed in the same story, but she said that we were Protestants and we did not wear crosses or have statues in our homes or in our churches. And that was that.

Maria was nice about it though and told me, "You can come visit our nativity scene whenever you like. I'm sure my mother won't mind."

She felt sorry for me, she said, "Because God likes Catholics best, and the reason you don't have a dad or any brothers or sisters is probably because you are a Protestant."

I began to argue. "I do have a dad. He's just not here."

But that's when I heard my mother's voice exclaim, "What are you doing here?" I wondered why she sounded so upset.

"Did you close the front door?" she asked in a voice that sounded angry.

I was not sure. "I think so." I suddenly felt as if I had done something terribly wrong, but was not sure what.

"Oh, my God!" She rushed downstairs.

I heard her scream as she ran into our apartment through the front hall ahead of me. "Oh, God, oh, my God! My God!"

Her bicycle that stood in the front hall had vanished. Her only winter coat that hung on the coatrack behind the bicycle was also gone.

"Oh, God, no!" my mother cried. "My identity card!"

It was then I realized that I had left the door not just unlocked, but wide open, so anyone who entered the portico that opened to the steps down to the street as well as to the four doors that led to six separate apartments would have easily spotted the bicycle. In this time of desperate hunger, a bicycle might buy a loaf of bread or a potato on the black market. Which of our neighbors had seen it and taken the opportunity? Who had betrayed us this time?

An accusing voice in my head said, *It was you. You left the door wide open. It is your fault.*

"My identity card! Oh, my God! Oh, my God!" My mother's voice echoed again as she paced up and down the hallway. "My identity card!"

My mother's identity card had been in the pocket of the coat that had been stolen. To risk being stopped on the streets of Amsterdam by the Gestapo without being able to show your identity card was to risk death or deportation to a camp.

I knew that. Every child my age already knew that.

My mother's panic-filled cries hurt my ears, and I desperately wished to make them go away. The fear and accusation in her voice made me want to hide and explain to her that I had not meant to leave the door open, but I could tell she did not want to hear me. For the first time in my young life, I experienced the emotion of knowing I had caused pain to someone I loved and on whose happiness I depended. I had put that person in danger, and there was nothing, absolutely nothing I could do to take the pain back or undo my part in it. It was my first remembered experience of guilt and remorse, and the crushing weight of it felt unbearably immense.

"Oh no, Mommy, I am so sorry!" I cried in a desperate attempt to get her to stop pacing. I wanted to convince myself that I had done nothing wrong. Of course her coat was still there. Everything was just fine, I wanted to say, and I squeezed my eyes tight to make it so, but my squeezing caused the room to spin, and I could not utter a word.

Then I felt my mother shaking me by my shoulders. "It's going to be all right. It will be all right."

I heard her words, but I did not want to open my eyes. I needed her to put her arms around me and hold me till we were both safe, but instead she held a glass of water to my mouth and told me to drink it. I thought I was going to throw up, but there was nothing in my belly to throw up, so I drank the water. Even so the tears behind my eyeballs kept forcing my eyes to stay shut.

That evening I could not sleep. I prayed to God, the big Father God that my mother said loved us, and begged him, "Please, please, please get my mom a new identity card." I told him that it was not her fault that it got stolen. It was mine.

"I am so very, very sorry," I said and wondered if God heard you if you admitted that you had made a very bad mistake. I wished I were Catholic like Maria. She had told me that Catholics went to something called confession where the priest heard you, even if God didn't, and after confession you never ever had to feel guilty about anything, even though I knew she was mean to her sisters sometimes. But I feared that what I had done was much worse than being mean to your sisters, and God would probably never give me a sister of my own now.

My mother could not sleep either, and we got up early to walk the many blocks across town to the Administrative Office where she would have to apply for a new card. She explained to me that she would have to be fingerprinted and photographed, but after that we walked in complete silence, and I would always remember that I felt very small and very bad and for some reason could not feel my legs.

At the first bridge crossing, a group of German soldiers who were engaged in a loud conversation blocked the sidewalk. I held my breath, certain that one of them would step toward us and tell my mother "Halt" or "Heil Hitler" and demand to see her identity card. But they barely looked our way. As we walked by them without being stopped, my breath exhaled hard. On the next street, a lone German soldier sauntered toward us, his gun slung over his shoulder as he looked my mother up and down. I wanted to cross the street to the other side, but my mother grabbed my arm with a tight painful grip and kept walking past him without any incident.

We finally made it to the Administrative Office in the historic building that in the sixteenth century had housed the orphans of Amsterdam. My mother was told to wait. I could see her shivering without her coat, and I felt myself shiver along with her.

After a long wait, a male clerk called my mother to a high counter where he began the bureaucratic process of interrogating, finger-printing, and photographing her. I stood next to her, holding on to her skirt, my face at eye level to the counter, and listened to the man lecturing my mother about her "carelessness" in not guarding such an important document as her identity card with more vigilance.

"Do you realize that you could have ended up in a concentration camp?" he asked, and then scolded her. "You'd better not make such a stupid mistake again, because next time you may not be so lucky."

I wanted to yell at him, "It was not my mother's fault. It was my fault," but I knew my mother would not want me to interrupt. It would not be polite.

After being instructed to fill out numerous forms, my mother was photographed and issued a temporary pass. Days later when we returned for the permanent one, I saw her shake her head at the new photo of her sunken face.

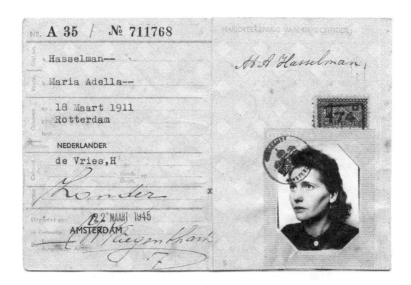

I wanted to tell her, "It will be all right, Mommy. We will be safe," the way that she always told me. But I felt too guilty. It had all been my fault. How could I know that I would not do something like that again? If I could make mistakes so easily, then how could I ever trust myself?

My mother tried to reassure me that she did not blame me. It was a mistake and she should not have left me alone. She proceeded to remind me that the reason we needed God was because we human beings always make mistakes. She called them "sins."

She then said, "Remember, God loves you."

She did not understand that I did not want God to love me when I made a mistake. I wanted her to love me, and I wanted God to help me not make mistakes in the first place. I wondered why this God that my mother and others seemed to know so intimately made human beings who could be careless and dangerous to the people they loved. A link to something secure inside of me had been broken. The one who was not to be trusted was not just the Nazi soldier or the Dutch betrayer out there. I had discovered there was someone inside of me who was capable of making hurtful mistakes, and I was not sure if I could tolerate that. I was not that brave, strong girl I promised my daddy I would be. And that felt bad, very bad.

After the theft the days went by without incident, each day much the same as the one before but with a little less to eat. We slept most of the time and didn't have much to say to each other. At some point my mother even stopped talking about God or reminding me to say my prayers.

She just said, "We cannot trust anyone anymore, because everyone around us is starving and desperate."

And one day she said out loud, "I am not sure the Allies will make it in time."

When I asked her about that, she said she didn't mean it, but her long silences made me think she did.

Then one morning there was an abrupt change. I was still rubbing the sleep out of my eyes when my mother nudged me awake with unusual energy and told me in a loud excited voice that she had one of her "good dreams." We had always told each other our dreams, or mostly always except for the one that I kept a secret.

And my mom proceeded to tell me her dream.

*In her dream my mother is asleep in bed when she is awakened by a special knock on the front door. It is a secret knock that only she, my dad, and the members of the resistance know. It is a Tuesday night, and when she opens the door, she sees my dad standing there. He looks strong and healthy. He hugs her and tells her that he was liberated from the German POW camp by American troops when Amsterdam was still occupied. It has taken him a long time to get home because he had to travel through the liberated south of the Netherlands to get to us, but he is home for good now.*

Her face flushed, my mother looked at me with a big smile that I had not seen for a long time now.

"Isn't that a wonderful dream, Henny? I know that God sent me that dream to let me know Daddy is alive. You'll see, he will be home soon, and we will have all the food we want." She gave me a bony hug and reassured me again, or maybe she was reassuring herself. "We will survive."

I believed her. I always tried to make myself believe her, but I did not tell her of my own dream that had come to me many nights now. I don't know why I never told her.

In my dream: *I am standing precariously close to the edge of a black, deep whirlpool. I am looking down into the swirling, dark waters and can feel myself almost falling in. I know very clearly in the dream that if I fall in, the cold, dark water will just spin and spin and spin and suck me down into its depths where I will be no more. I begin to fall. . . .* Then I wake up.

I always woke up just as I could feel myself begin to fall. I thought that was probably a good thing.

# Chapter 18

# Liberation

The day Amsterdam was finally liberated should have been a day that I would always remember with joy. It certainly started out that way on the morning of May 7 when my mother and I woke up.

May had arrived a week before with warm spring weather and the welcome word on the street and among our neighbors that the war in the rest of Holland had officially been declared over. Tragically, the city of Amsterdam in the still-occupied western provinces remained under German siege, and most of its inhabitants by now literally had nothing left to eat. In a desperate attempt to save the starving population, the Allies were engaged in a project called "Operation Manna" through which food parcels were being dropped over the occupied territory from low-flying bombers. The arrival of the promised bombardment of cans of milk powder and soups, boxes of crackers, and other desperately needed nourishment was awaited with much hope and anticipation. For many people, however, help would come too late.

"All we can do now is wait," my mother said.

Starved and tyrannized into submission, we had become a city of people for whom waiting was the only action left. We were waiting for the Allies to liberate us. We were waiting for food supplies to drop out of planes and be distributed. We were waiting for loved ones to come home. We were waiting for the return of civility and kindness, waiting for the streets to ring once again with cordial greetings and joyful laughter that could reanimate the inner deadness that had wormed its way through our empty bellies into our souls. And so with not a single crumb of food left in the kitchen cupboards, we waited.

Then suddenly on a lovely Monday morning, the days, weeks, and years of waiting came to an end. My mother and I awakened to loud unusual noises: raucous sounds of laughter and jubilant singing that came up from the street outside and below our bedroom window. My mom opened the window and leaned out.

Neighbors shouted up to her from the street in excited voices, "The Allied Forces have arrived! Amsterdam has been liberated! The war is over! We are all going to the Dam Square. There is going to be a parade and a celebration. Come join us."

"The Allies have arrived. We are free! We are free!" My mother repeated the words to me, pensive for a moment, and then added, "Did you hear that, honey? The war is over! We are free, free, free!" Tears wet her smiling, sunken face.

"Come on, we are going to go to the Dam."

The Dam was the name of the square that fronted the Royal Palace, a good ten-minute walk from our home, even for healthy, well-fed bodies, and certainly daunting for our starved ones, but that did not seem to bother my mother.

I didn't quite know how to respond to her tears and smiles as she rushed me to put on my shoes with the slits in the front, wash my face with the cold water from the icy faucet, comb my hair, and brush my teeth, without toothpaste of course. We had not seen toothpaste for a long, long time. But my mother never let me leave the house without washing my face and hands, and combing my hair. She always believed that as long as we kept ourselves clean, it meant we wanted to stay alive. And the icy cold water was good for me, she told me, because it would make my skin glow and be beautiful for the rest of my life. I believed her. I always believed her, or at least I tried to.

The moment we left the house and headed toward the Dam or Palace Square, my mother's legs seemed to move into high speed. It was as if all her exhaustion had left her, and she could almost fly. My spindly, seven-year-old legs had to move faster than I could make them to keep up with the long-distance speed walker and running champion that had suddenly resurfaced in my mother's starved body.

*How could she walk so fast?* I wondered, feeling angry and wanting her to slow down and stop pulling me.

"Come on, Henny," she urged, ignoring my resistance as she dragged me along by my arm.

Within minutes it seemed we had covered the many blocks of cobblestoned streets and bridges to reach the square in front of the queen's palace where a jubilant crowd had already gathered. We were met by the sounds of people singing. Some had hooked arms and were dancing with laughing abandonment. Total strangers addressed each other with hugs and smiles, shouting, "Freedom at last!" They sang "Oranje boven," "Orange above all," as they celebrated the color of the Dutch monarchy without fear of Nazi reprisal. Some in the crowd carried orange banners or scarves, while others waved the national Dutch red, white, and blue flag. My mother hooked arms with other dancers, and I felt my small body being swept along on a wave of energy that I could not identify. I had no previous experience of such a collective surge of joy. It caused me to be giddy in a way that felt both pleasurable and at the same time a little scary.

One older man grabbed both my hands and twirled me around. "Hey, girly, you are free. Do you know what that means, little girl? Smile! Smile, little girl! You are free! Free!"

My feet didn't touch the ground, and I saw my mom join in his exuberance as he gently put me down and placed a kiss on her cheek. "We are free!" he roared as he moved on to grab the next person's arm.

Perhaps if someone had been able to take a photo at that moment, this serious little girl might have shown a smile on her face. Who knows? I would always vaguely remember my mother and I both laughing out loud for the first time in many months. We surrendered control and allowed ourselves to be swept up by the collective euphoria. Our voices joined with others in the rising triumphant singsong roar of "Freedom! Freedom!"

Then all of a sudden, without warning, deafening staccato sounds popped the joyous air of song and celebration.

"Gunshots!" someone yelled as shots exploded in rapid succession *tack-tack-tack* from somewhere over our heads.

Sounds of screams and gunshots pummeled my ears. People started pushing, yelling, and running. A woman fell down so near to us that I saw her face twist in pain and shock. A little boy cried, "Mama, Mama!" and I watched the dark red blood gush out of his mother's head and form a pattern around the stones on the ground. Hypnotized, I froze in place. My mother yanked my arm. Someone picked up the boy whose cries of "Mama, Mama!" continued to mix with the screams and the gunshots. We ran into a street looking for safety, my mother dragging me along by my arm.

Unlike my mother's legs, mine were never made for running, and I had no idea they could move this fast, but they did. My arm was twisted in pain, its skin burning from my mother's relentless grip as she pulled me behind a pillar and covered my body with hers. From the corner of my eyes I saw soldiers running by with guns flaring.

"Quick, this way!" A man waved to us after the first soldiers had passed us, and we ran behind him into another small side street on our left. He ducked behind a pile of rubble in a vacant lot and motioned us to join him. My mom hesitated. Even in that horrific moment of choice, I could see her reaching into that still place within herself where she had always weighed things to make decisions.

She shook her head and dragged me along behind her again. A woman waved us into her upstairs apartment. My mother nodded.

Several other people followed us up the stairs.

Within seconds we heard more gunshots and glass shattering. "Stay away from the windows!" a man in the room warned in a brusque voice.

The little boy whose mother had been shot huddled beside me under the dining room table where the adults had pushed us children away from the windows.

He continued his cries of "Mama, Mama . . . Mama!"

I wanted him to stop. He made me remember the flowing patterns of blood on the ground where she had fallen down next to us. I didn't want to hear the screams or his cries. My mother crouched down next to the table and took my hand. With her other hand she stroked the little boy's head. She did not tell him that everything would be all right, but he stopped crying anyway. Later another woman took him into her arms. That made me glad. I would dream of him in later years and wonder what became of him. I never even knew his name. And I would also remember the little girl with the rag doll and question, "Why them and why not me?" and be diagnosed with "survivor guilt."

After a short time, the shooting stopped. Dutch voices outside announced that the Germans had been captured. It was safe to come out now. My mother and I left the apartment building and walked by the vacant lot. A bloodied body lay sprawled out across the rubble. By his clothing, I recognized the body as the man who had motioned us to join him. My mother started to put her hands over my eyes again, but I pushed them away. I could look for myself. I came to my own awareness that day that she and I would have been dead also if we had joined him. A cold jolt of anger shot through my small body, and then all sound disappeared.

For the rest of my life I would remember the eerie silence of our slow walk home. It was as if I had been wrapped in a sealed-off bubble, a bubble of silence from which all worldly sound had been sucked out. Like someone in a dreamscape, my eyes could see the buildings we passed, my legs could move one after the other to make my body walk, and my lungs were able to pump the air I needed to breathe in and out, but they all operated in a soundless bubble. I walked in a void, a vacuum where no sound existed or could penetrate.

When we reached our apartment, my mother unlocked the door, and we stepped inside. With a gesture of deliberation, she closed the door behind us as if she could finally shut out the horrors of the war for good.

"Enough. Enough. We are safe," she whispered in a voice that seemed to come from a great distance away.

The apartment enveloped us in its cold and hollow emptiness. I felt a vague longing for someone to greet and comfort us, a kind reassuring voice or a touch of human warmth to bring us back to ourselves. The image of Mr. Sleumer's comforting appearance on the back steps after I discovered my mother smashing the radios entered wisp-like into my bubble like a ghost who seemed just within reach but then disappeared. My dad, Nel, Mr. Sleumer—all felt like dream figures from such a long, long time ago.

My mother muttered as if speaking to herself, "Not even hot water or tea to make a cup of tea. Not even a cup of tea." Her words barely grazed my bubble.

We collapsed together into the big, old, overstuffed armchair in the living room. I felt the trembling in both our bodies as her hard, knobby bones pressed against mine, and I wondered if we were now going to die. I drifted off into the other world, the world of my ever-present imagination where mystery and possibility mingled with what might be real, and I pictured my daddy coming home and finding us in his old chair, two skeletons in a locked embrace. He would be so sad, so very sad, I thought.

Then suddenly, as if remembering herself, my mother spoke, her voice louder this time. "Remember, Henny, the war is over. We are safe. Daddy is coming home."

I barely heard her words.

She ranted on, "The Allies have already dropped big parcels of food outside Amsterdam. We will have something to eat soon. We really are safe! It's over!" She burst into tears and folded me in her arms.

The rising fierceness of her voice pushed her words through the silence and dissolved the bubble that still surrounded me. She hugged me so tight against her that I could hear her heartbeat, and as surely as if I were back in her womb, I drew from that maternal life force to nourish my own.

I believed her then as I had always believed her. I had to. If I didn't, I was certain that my body would break into a thousand pieces and I would fall into that dark vortex of the swirling waters in my nightly dream. She was my rock. I believed she had a direct line to God, who told her everything would be all right. I believed her dreams and intuition, I clung to her thin strong body that day, and I sucked that strength, faith, and knowing deep into my lungs and made it mine.

As I grew older, it would take deep therapy to differentiate myself from that fierce mother who gave me her strength, courage, and faith. We would do battle, she and I, as I struggled to find my own identity separate from hers. I would discover that there were many ways in which I was more like my father. But whenever I was confronted by life's inevitable challenges, she would be right there, a fierce internalized mother who nudged me on and told me that everything would turn out all right, somehow, and I would believe her because I felt her strength, determination, and resilience inside of me.

We did not have anything to eat that evening, but the two slices of gluey bread lay securely in the orange pan for the following morning. We would survive, my mother promised.

# Chapter 19

# The Lucky Ones

An insistent knocking sound startled me out of a restless sleep. For the second night after my mother and I had made our way home from the deadly shooting on the Palace Square, we had gone to bed without anything to eat except for the slice of bread made out of tulip bulbs that we had devoured to the last bitter bite that morning. With the war and Nazi occupation now over, well-nourished friendly Canadian soldiers had begun to replace the hostile presence of the threatening Gestapo bullies in the streets of Amsterdam. On the surface the horror of it all was finally over, but many people in our battered city were still starving to death. Food distribution had become tangled in bureaucracy, and the joyful exuberance of young people mingling in the streets with the Canadian liberators hid the lingering impact of trauma, malnutrition, and starvation that continued to claim its victims behind the closed doors of many homes.

*Knock, knock . . . knock*, I heard it again. *Knock, knock . . . knock!* I sat upright in bed; my heart jumped so hard that I could feel it thumping against my ribs. I resisted the urge to scream "No! Not again!" But this time there were no threatening voices commanding that we "open the door," and I did not hear any splintering sound of someone kicking down the back door in our kitchen. My mother had already climbed out of bed. I rubbed the sleep out of my eyes and stumbled after her out the bedroom and through the hallway as she walked to the front door.

She opened the door, and I looked up at the tall male figure standing in the doorway. It was my father. My mother threw herself into his arms with a squeal of joy, as he stepped forward across the threshold and took up all the space in our tiny front hall.

"Oh Hein, oh Hein!" my mother repeated again and again. They held each other in an embrace that I thought lasted forever.

I hid behind her. His invasive presence seemed to suck all the air out of the hallway. I could not breathe. For the past six months, the only other living being besides me in our apartment had been the malnourished presence of my petite mother. This tall well-fed soldier in the khaki American uniform loomed too big, too powerful.

I had no feelings for this man hugging my mother. He had no place in the story of my mother's and my traumatized life. He was not there when the Nazis broke into our home, held a gun at my mother's head, and dragged away Nel. He was not there when the hunger and cold made death a constant companion on our cobblestoned streets of Amsterdam. He was not there when enemy soldiers shot at us and splattered the ground with bodies and blood on the day we celebrated our liberation.

"It's Daddy," my mother said, and I brushed her away. I knew that this man was my father. I did not need her to tell me that. The problem was that I could not access the feelings of joy she wanted me to express. I could not feel anything at all.

Like two strangers, he and I stared at each other across a chasm of years and separate traumas. He did not try to reach out to me and I did not step forward to hug him. My mother pulled me gently toward him. "It's Daddy," she said again. I pushed through my numb passivity to please her. I looked up at him and ostensibly said, "You have grown."

He looked down at me and said in a gruff voice, "So have you."

My mother took us both by the hand and led us into the living room where I leaned against her, still standing, while they sat down on opposite chairs. He held her hands and stared at my mother's gaunt face and our starved bodies as he kept repeating the words "Goddammit! I had no idea. I had no idea. Goddammit!"

I recoiled at the rough repetition of the swear words uttered in his guttural male voice. My memory of him had excluded the gruff masculinity of my father's speech pattern that sounded so much like the harsh commanding voices of the German soldiers that had controlled and threatened our lives.

"When is the last time you two had something to eat?" he asked my mother in a brusque tone.

"It doesn't matter," my mother whispered through her tears. "The war is over and you are home."

"Tomorrow morning first thing I am going to get you something to eat. I promise you. Tomorrow," he repeated, "tomorrow you start eating again. Goddammit! I promise you."

I heard his words, but I didn't believe him, and I still could not feel anything. I would later remember that it was as if I were watching a movie. I was an observer and not a participant in my parents' happy reunion. That is, until he reached into his pocket and, leaning toward me, carefully placed something in my hand.

"I think this is yours," he said with a smile, his voice softened.

I looked at the squashed tiny thing he had put in my hands. A flattened remainder of a small toy dog, its skin torn, its straw insides all but gone, its red color faded, it barely hung together as a piece of faded cloth. I looked up into the face of the man who was my father and felt my chest heave. Imprisoned feelings escaped from the dark pit below and pushed their way to the surface. "My little red dog," I whispered.

His gaze intent on mine, he said: "The wolf. He took care of me, just like you said he would. Do you remember that?"

I nodded. "Yes. Yes." Tears blurring my sight of him, I blinked.

"He saved my life," he said. He stretched out his arms, "Come here," and lifted me onto his lap.

Clutching the remains of the tiny toy dog that I had handed the German guard two years earlier, I laid my head against my father's shoulder. My face brushed the coarse fabric of his military uniform where I felt the wetness of my own tears, and I surrendered.

"Daddy, Daddy, you have come home." I sobbed and wrapped my arms around my daddy's neck.

"Yes, I have," he said and pulled me close to him.

My starved small body at long last yielded to its deep fatigue. Tonight I did not have to be a "brave girl." Tonight I could just be a child.

My parents carried me to their bed and tucked me in between them for the remainder of the night. For the first time in many years, the muffled voices of my mother and father in conversation lulled me gently into a deep sleep, a lullaby of peace.

While I slept, my father told my mother that he had been liberated from the German prison camp by American troops weeks earlier, exactly as she had seen in her dream. He had traveled with them to Amsterdam through the southern parts of the Netherlands that had already been set free by the Allies. Though he knew that Amsterdam was still occupied by the Germans, he had no knowledge of the extent of the Hunger Winter and the famine that had ravaged the city. He was totally unprepared for the two skeletal beings that awaited him when he arrived on our doorstep that evening. Early the next morning, true to his word, wearing the US uniform and insignia given him by the American troops, my father claimed his status as a Dutch war veteran and former prisoner of war to gain entry into the barracks of the Canadian liberators stationed in Amsterdam. He demanded that he be given food immediately for his starving wife and child. His act probably saved our lives. While food supplies had by now arrived in Amsterdam to be distributed to its starving population, bureaucracy persisted in stalling the distributions. Thousands continued to suffer and die from malnutrition for days and even weeks after the liberation. My father saw that we could not wait. When medics checked my mother's and my physical condition several days after my father's return, we were diagnosed to have been just a few weeks away from death by starvation.

But on this morning with my father's big, strong hand securely holding mine, I did what I had done those many, many years ago before he left; I tried to match my steps to his as we walked along the cobblestoned canal street across the nearby square toward the hastily constructed barracks for the Canadian liberating troops. When we arrived at the barracks, the joviality of the young Canadian soldiers' voices threatened to overwhelm me. I did not understand the English language in which they and my dad communicated, and I grasped my dad's hand tighter. In response he lifted me up off the ground and held me snug in his arms. Danger and pleasure, danger and pleasure, flashed alternate blinking lights in my brain when one of the uniformed Canadian soldiers reached out to me and told my dad that he also had a little girl my age at home. When my dad translated his English into Dutch, I asked him if she had enough to eat. The soldier showed me her picture and said that yes she did. He then added in his best Dutch with a big smile, "And you will too." The soldiers continued to make a fuss of me. They also warned me to be careful and not eat too much straightaway, because my body needed time to get used to absorbing food again. We were given a container of soup, a pack of soda crackers, and a very large can of powdered milk.

In later years I would remember being shown the photo of the Canadian soldier's little girl, and I would think of the little Jewish girl who had dropped her doll, and the little boy on the Palace Square whose mother's blood formed patterns on the ground that could still make my stomach feel queasy. And then I would hear about Anne Frank, who lived just a few blocks from my home, and later again read a book by a friend who grew up German as a young girl amid the bombing of Berlin, and all the pictures of the little children will mingle into one child's face, one child to represent all the children scarred by what one of my future teachers, the archetypal psychologist James Hillman, would refer to as humanity's "terrible love of war."

However, on this particular day, I remember walking home from the Canadian barracks with my father's firm hand still holding mine. And when I looked around at the men and women who passed by us, I wanted to shout, "This is my daddy. We have food!" But my dad and I walked in silence as we always did so many years before, and when we arrived at our apartment, we sat down quietly at the dining room table. My mother gave thanks, and then we chewed slowly on the crackers and sipped a small glass of milk made with milk powder. I let the silky milk flow slowly over my tongue and fill my mouth with its sweetness. My teeth crunched down on the crackers made with real flour. We were the lucky ones. We had survived the Hunger Winter.

# Chapter 20

# Grief and Celebration

"This is not my city! Not the same city! It will never be the same again!"

My father's voice trembled with such an agonizing mix of grief and anger on that sunny afternoon that even just remembering the shock of it could immobilize me with feelings of unbearable sadness well into my adult years.

My parents and I had just passed the Mint Tower on a long walk through the city center. An unusually sparkling day, the streets of Amsterdam bustled with the lively sights and sounds of our Canadian liberators, young men armed with cigarettes, chewing gum, and stockings, who brought out the flirtatious laughter of the Dutch girls they charmed. Optimism and the eternal energetic renewal of youth danced on the warm spring air. The long wait for freedom over, loved ones who had been in hiding elsewhere in the country or imprisoned in the German camps had begun to return to their homes one by one, but for every story with a happy ending, there was a story of loss, of loved ones who returned maimed or never came home. For many people in our old city, the grieving process had barely begun.

After years of separation and individual struggles for survival, both the people who had been waiting and the ones who
returned faced adjustments and new challenges for which no one
had prepared them, challenges that would test their already thinly
stretched resilience and endurance. My parents, in their own
unique attempt to recreate the life they had shared before their
two-year separation and individual war experiences, began to
retrace their footsteps along old familiar paths through the city
they both loved. After all, even though they had met in Rotterdam,
they had begun their married life in Amsterdam, where as a young
couple they had discovered a shared passion for the romantic old
center of this city and enjoyed leisurely strolls along its tree-lined
canals and through its historic neighborhoods with its many cafés.
This was the city where they had chosen to start our family and
where my father had created the small business that had led to his
deep friendships with the Jewish men and their wives whom we
used to visit when I was a much littler girl.

My parents had already revisited the neighborhood that once held
the vibrant Jewish heart of that Amsterdam. They walked along the
familiar streets near the Portuguese Synagogue and to the market
square, the Waterlooplein, where my father had spent much of his
time before his imprisonment in Germany. But my mother told me
that, at the sight of the homes that now stood empty and boarded up
or were occupied by strangers, my father had choked up with grief
and said to her, "They are all gone. This is no longer my city."

And that evening when he and my mother were deep in discussion and I had gone to bed and he thought I was asleep, I heard him
swear, "Those bastards! They murdered them all! It will never be the
same!"

I buried my head under the blankets and fell into a restless sleep
in which I dreamed that I could not find either my mother or my
father, so you can imagine my relief when my mother woke me up

in the morning and told me that it was "a beautiful sunny day," and we would take a walk through a part of town with "fewer memories."

"It will be good for us. People will be out and about there to celebrate the liberation," she said.

And when my father remained silent at the breakfast table, she stressed in that resolute voice of hers that I had come to know so well, "We need to celebrate our freedom!"

But the jubilant atmosphere of the young celebrating the country's liberation on that sparkling day could not lift my father's spirits. In his grief, the festivities only seemed to magnify for him the horrors that had been committed.

"This is not my city! Not the same city! It will never be the same again!" His deep trembling voice hid a howling scream, and my heart would never forget the piercing shock of his anguish.

He was right, of course. The liberation had freed us, but it could not bring back the innocent victims whose lives had been so brutally extinguished. Most of the friends my father had come to know and care about through his work would never return from the concentration camps. We would never again see the kind uncles in whose homes I had fallen asleep on my daddy's lap to the sound of the comforting voices of their jovial camaraderie.

And it scared me to hear him say again to my mother on the way home from that sunny day's walk, "What's the point! It's no use! Things will never be the same."

But my mother just said, "We must try. The war is over, and you are home."

Then he sighed and nodded.

And I put my hand in his so I could feel safe.

Expressions of joy and grief got all mixed up in those early days and weeks after the liberation of our city. On the surface the horrors of the war and the cruelties of the Nazi Regime now lay behind us. The Allies had won, our country was free, and we were expected to be out celebrating with jubilation. But behind closed doors within the homes and hearts of many of the survivors, the pain and suffering caused by the brutal regime had not yet come to a stop by any means.

And as my father suppressed his grief and joined the other men, who had returned home, to look for work that could provide financial security and safety for their families, I would continue to learn more about the emotional strength of women.

# Chapter 21

# The Women—
# Unfinished Stories

With the return of the men, the housewives, who, in their absence, had shouldered the burdens of raising the children in the daily fight for survival, now drew on whatever emotional resources they had left to help those families who mourned or could not cope.

The neighbor girl Hedi, whose mother and mine had once ridden their bicycles into the farmlands to get us the few potatoes that may have staved off our starvation, renewed our friendship as our mothers, the former heroic "hunger trippers," joined neighborhood housewives in their spontaneous groups of outreach. Instead of tricking German guards, our mothers now served cups of tea; stroked the forehead of the mother a few doors down who could not stop screaming after her son was returned in a coffin, his legs twisted into his belly as a result of torture and punishment for his activity in the resistance; and held the hands of the other mother whose son had come home with gangrene in his foot that would necessitate the amputation of his leg. Some of the men and women they tended had returned home with wounds in places that did not show, survivors who could not weep or tell their stories in words because the atrocities they experienced had buried themselves like shrapnel in their soul if not their flesh and bones. Others would never return, leaving behind loved ones who needed permission to mourn. The housewives in their print dresses just listened and offered up words of hope and sympathy with their cups of tea. And sometimes, as with the young girl whose fiancé had betrayed her to join the Nazi movement, they chided that it was time to "get on with life."

But in their tending to grief, they did not ignore those whose stories had happy endings that called for expressions of joy. In those days before public television or social media, it was the women in our neighborhood who circulated the news of the families that had been reunited, of atrocities and unimaginable challenges endured and survived, and they made sure to broadcast the acts of fortitude and moral courage as well as happy outcomes that they deemed deserving of communal recognition and celebration.

One afternoon when I arrived home from school, I heard the excited chatter and laughter of women on the stairway that led to the apartments above ours. Since my mother was not at home, I assumed she and the other housewives were exchanging their news for the day, so I did not pay much attention.

Then all of a sudden a familiar voice called down to me: "Henny! Hennepiet!"

I turned my head and looked up into the twinkling dark eyes of a pale, thin-faced young woman with a totally shaven head.

My heart exploded. "Nel? Nel? Oh, Nel! You are bald!"

We grabbed each other's arms on the stairs while I babbled inanely about her shaven head and couldn't stop prattling, "Where is your beautiful hair? Your hair?"

She laughed out loud. "It'll grow back," she said and hugged me again.

I felt the wetness of the tears on our faces as we clung to each other. "You are home," I gasped. "You are alive! You are alive!" Suddenly I experienced an old familiar sensation of fear. What was she doing out in the open on the stairs where everyone could see her? I wanted to hide her, to make her safe. My mind needed time to absorb the shock of seeing her for the very first time in my life outside the confines of our apartment. How could she be safe?

"What is going on?" I heard my mother's voice call up from the street below us. "Nel? Nel? Nel! You're alive! Oh, thank God! Thank God!"

Laughing while tears wet her cheeks, she embraced Nel and quickly unlocked the front door to our apartment.

"Come in, come in quick," she said, pushing us inside.

And I experienced a sense of relief when my mother closed the door and the three of us huddled together in the safety of our living room, just as we had in a time that now seemed so very long ago, as if it belonged to another world. We cried, we hugged, we babbled, and I seemed to remember that my mother made us tea.

I felt strangely disoriented though. Old fears were not that easily set aside. As if caught in a time bubble, my chest tightened and the image of Nel being dragged out from under my mother's bed flashed before me. My mind struggled as it tried to catch up to the reality of her freedom. My mom noticed and tapped me on my arm as she sometimes did when she observed my spacing out. She called it my "leaving," which I did from time to time. Her touch always brought me back.

"What happened after you were taken away from us?" she asked Nel. "Can you tell us or was it all too horrible? Would you rather not? We've heard such horrific things about those death camps. Oh, Nel! Nel! But you are safe now! That's what is important! Thank God!"

The peculiar selectivity of memory would often perplex me. I noticed how I recalled with ease the smells, sounds, and especially the emotions of important events but forgot whole chunks of narrative. For the rest of my life, I would remember the deep emotional joy at seeing Nel on those stairs and the shock of her shaven head, but I would remember little of the story she told us about herself, and perhaps, after all, that's how it should be. That was her story, not mine, to tell. We would all learn to live with our unfinished life narratives from those days. But what I would remember, and the way my mother retold it to me many times, was as follows:

> *After being dragged from our home, Nel was put on a train to a concentration camp. I never knew which one, but upon her arrival at the camp, she was herded into a space where she and others were separated into two lines. The prisoners were not told how the lines differed, but as she watched closely, she noticed that the people who looked strong and healthy were directed into one line and those who looked weak, were old, had troubling standing, or wore eyeglasses were shoved into the other line. Nel could not see much without her eyeglasses, but at that moment she tossed them and proceeded to join the line of those who looked strong and healthy and of whom none wore eyeglasses. This act probably saved her life, for when the monstrous barbarism of the Nazi concentration camps became public, we learned of course that the men and women who were judged to be weak, old, or imperfect were immediately murdered in the gas chambers. Those who were judged strong, young, and healthy enough to work were granted a reprieve. A healthy young woman could still be used to serve the Third Reich for a little longer.*

My secret stepsister had survived the unspeakable, and so had my mother and I. We did not share the rest of our stories, neither the concentration camp horrors that Nel endured nor the torments of hunger or the terror of the shooting on the Palace Square that almost killed my mother and me. It was the way things were. The three of us had survived. That was all that mattered. Time to give thanks and move on.

We needed to focus on the future. "To have lingered in the past would have felt like a self-indulgent use of energy that we needed to recreate our lives," my mother would tell me in later years when I asked her why the stories were left untold.

The image of Nel lined up with other Holocaust victims on the way to the gas chambers and making her decision to surreptitiously discard her eyeglasses etched itself permanently in my brain alongside the imprint of hearing and seeing my mother make the decision not to reveal her involvement with the resistance movement to her Dutch Nazi interrogators. The images would always be my link to deep emotions of gratitude and enormous admiration. Under monstrous circumstances, these two women made deliberate life choices that helped them survive. They chose disobedience over submission, rational thought and action over passivity, and took control of their own destinies under threat of the most brutal authoritarian forces our world had seen. Their stories, as I experienced, recalled, and heard them, opened a crack through which the moral rightness and power of free, independent choice of thought and action for all human beings slipped into my young female brain.

As war transitioned into peace, the depth of grief and loss sustained among neighbors, friends, and relatives in our country became more apparent. But whether the neighbor who grieved the son she lost to torture, the wife whose husband succumbed to starvation in the final days of the Hunger Winter, the father who bore witness to a community of friends extinguished from a city that would "never be the same," or those who returned from atrocities that could not be spoken, the full stories remained mostly untold. Theirs were the unfinished stories of war that would not be shared until decades later when new lives had been reimagined and created.

"Best to forget now. Time to look to the future. Let the past be," my mother repeated. "Let's remember the stories with happy endings."

And she would remind me of the warmth and the light that returned, the "miracle" of the full moon on the dark, icy New Year's night.

"Daddy is home, Nel is alive. We must thank God," my mother said.

That afternoon, after another hug, I watched Nel walk out our front door. A young woman in charge of her own life, she said good-bye to the place and time that demanded she hide to save her life. Fear clutched at my chest momentarily when she walked away.

"It's all right," my mother said as she took my hand. "She is safe now."

The words hung in the air between us. "She is safe now."

Four simple words that carried such phenomenal power! In future years I would wonder if there might ever be a time when we could say about every young person on our planet, "She is safe now." How amazing that would be.

For now the flames of hatred and prejudice that had engulfed the world for the past five years had been extinguished and my mother could reassure me.

"She is safe now," she said again, her voice firm, as if after a job well done.

But I was a child of that war, and as Nel, my secret stepsister, walked away from us into her new life, and my father shared my mother's bed behind a closed door in the evenings, I missed being in my stepsister's arms or in the warm bed I had shared with my mother. I felt lonely, until my dad handed me the care of another.

# Chapter 22

# "Something to Care For . . ."

W hen my parents were called into my school because I had punched a classmate and given her a bloody nose, they realized that I was in real trouble. My teacher had praised me in front of the class for my good grades that morning when that girl taunted me in the playground and said, "You think you are so smart, so special, it's just because you are an only child." She spat out the words "only child" as if it was something shameful and I flung myself at her. I couldn't help myself, especially after she'd been prattling on about her wonderful brothers and sisters the whole week.

Things weren't that great at home either. My mother had caught me eating spoonfuls of strawberry jam out of the jar again, after she had already told me twice that the jar was to last the family for the next three or four weeks. She had also stored the large can of dry milk powder on a high shelf in the kitchen where she thought it would be safely out of my reach, but it was an easy climb on a chair, and from there onto the kitchen counter to get it down. I had made myself several glasses of milk and even gobbled down three or four heaping spoonfuls of the sweet-tasting powder just dry out of the can before my mother noticed. At first she had been nice about it, but after I tore chunks out of the fresh bread she had bought for that day, she lost her patience and told me to sit on a chair in the corner of the room and that as a punishment we would not go to the movie that she and my dad had planned to take me to see.

Luckily she had not found out yet that the day before I had also stolen a cookie from the counter of the bakery and the baker had warned me that he would tell my parents that their daughter was "a thief." That did scare me and made me feel sorry, and I apologized to that baker without anyone ordering me.

I didn't like making my mom and dad unhappy, but I felt miserably lonely. My parents wondered if my being an only child accounted for my sleepwalking episodes in which I supposedly walked to our front door in the middle of the night, opened the hinged mail slot that opened to the outside, and called out to the little boy who lived across the portico to come out and play. He was two years younger than I was and had once told his mother that he was going to marry me when he grew up, but she had said that would never be possible. "Boys marry younger girls, never older girls," she admonished both of us, her voice filled with disdain. We had not played together since, and I had no idea why I would do such a strange thing as call him through the mail slot in the middle of the night, but then I didn't really know why I did any of the things that worried my parents so.

After meeting with the principal of my school and making me apologize to that horrible girl when I had to say, "I am really sorry I gave you a bloody nose," but really wanted to say, "I don't like you and don't ever call me an *only child* again as if it is a bad word, or I will punch you again," my dad told my mother that I needed something to care for and they should get me a puppy. I agreed with my mother that it was a terrible idea. I had not seen a live pet since we'd spied the black-and-white cat on the garden wall and eyed it as a possible meal and not a creature for company. My mother argued that she didn't think she had the strength to take care of a dog, especially a puppy, but my father insisted he would help and we should at least wander over to the open market that weekend to take a look. He had heard that farmers were bringing in litters of puppies from dogs that had survived outside of the urban areas, and he thought it would be a good thing for all of us to get reacquainted with animals again.

Though a city man, my father believed in nature as our teacher, and by the time I was barely two years old, he and my mother were taking me on regular visits to the Artis Zoo of Amsterdam, the oldest zoological gardens in the Netherlands, where under his guidance I learned to interact with donkeys, goats, and other farm animals in the children's petting zoo. In his respect for animals, he showed an instinctual understanding and natural connection with them, especially with horses and dogs, and had I known the term back then, I would probably have said that my father was a bit of "a horse or a dog whisperer."

But the last dog I remembered stroking before all the pets disappeared in the Hunger Winter was a big black Bouvier named Noir who belonged to one of our neighbors. I liked to hug and pet Noir and nuzzle my face in his thick fur, which had scared my mother. If I concentrated now, I could still feel his wet tongue on my cheeks and nose, licks that established the fact that Noir liked me, which his owner had said made me special because Noir had a tendency to bite children. I guess that is why my mother didn't approve of my running up to Noir and throwing my arms around his warm furry neck every time I saw him. He never once tried to bite me, though, but one day Noir disappeared, and two of the boys down the street told me that his owners had eaten him. My mom said that was not true, that he had to be put to sleep because there was no food to keep him alive.

"It was the kindest thing to do," she had said in her matter-of-fact war tone of voice.

Of course, everything was suddenly different now. Once food

became available again, people began to miss the love and companionship of pets. "Something to fill their hearts instead of their stom-
achs," my father said.

I guess my father managed to persuade my mother, because that
weekend we took off for our very long walk to the market on the
other side of town. When we arrived there, he immediately located
the stand where a farmer showed us the basket that held a pile of
wriggly, tan-colored, fat little puppies with bulbous noses and rolls of
velvety skin. There were five of them climbing all over each other in
every direction as they tumbled and yelped with each nudge.

"Oh, they're so sweet," I was surprised to hear my mother say, and
when she lifted one out of the basket and held it in her arms with a
big smile on her face, I became curious but stepped back in what had
become my usual stance of defiance: shoulders squared and pulled
up to my ears, mouth unsmiling. She held it out to me, but I watched
stone-faced and refused to touch it.

"Look, he is so sweet. Just hold him for a second," my mother tried
to coax me.

I took another step back and shook my head with a resolute no.

Then my dad asked me if I remembered how he taught me that
you could load and unload a camera in the dark by using only touch.

"Do you remember that?" he said.

I nodded, and I wondered what his camera had to do with a puppy.

"Do you think you could remember what a puppy's fur feels like
if you touched him with just your fingertips but your eyes remained
closed?" my dad asked.

I shrugged my shoulders.

"Are you willing to try?" he said.

I shrugged again. "I suppose."

"You have to close your eyes," he said.

I closed my eyes and he took one of my hands in his and guided
my fingers.

"Just feel him with only the tips of your fingers," he reminded me.

I allowed him to guide my hand and let my fingers very gently touch the puppy's fur. It felt warm, soft, and silky. Suddenly I experienced a series of quick, moist, little touches on the back of my hand. It shocked me but made me smile. Even with my eyes closed, I knew that it was the puppy's tongue. My dad asked me if I could hold out my arms but still keep my eyes closed.

I nodded yes, and felt my dad place the warm wriggling ball of fur in my arms as he moved my elbows and forearms so I could hold it firmly. It squirmed, and I held it closer to my chest. The puppy's warmth against my throat and neck released something tight and angry in me so that for a moment I relaxed my shoulders and, opening my eyes, saw a pink little tongue flick up to my chin.

"Keep your eyes closed and just feel him," my dad urged.

I closed my eyes again and could feel the puppy's tongue on my face.

"He likes me," I announced.

"I think he does," my dad said. "How about that!"

I continued to hold that warm furry body in my arms and let it lick my hands and face.

"Do you think you want to take him home?" my dad asked.

"Yes, I think so." I nodded and opened my eyes to take a closer look at the squirming little pup I was cuddling in my arms.

My dad then said that there was a serious condition and he wanted me to take my time and think about it. It had to be my own choice and if I really wanted this puppy, I would be totally responsible for him. I would have to promise to feed him, brush him, and take him for walks after school.

"I can do that," I said.

"There is another problem though." My dad sighed. "This little dog is way too small yet to walk the long distance to our house, so if you want him, you have to carry him all the way. And that is a long way."

I placed my cheek up against the warm little body of this wriggly pup that had not stopped licking me and at this point knew for sure that I was not about to let anyone take him away from me.

"But, oh yes," my dad added, "if you really want him, you also have to give him his name before you can take him home."

Tightening my hold on this lively little ball of fluff, I made my promises and promptly named him "little bear" or "Beertje" in Dutch, because he reminded me of pictures I had seen of cuddly bear cubs. On the long way home, that wriggly pup became heavier and heavier, but the warmth of his furry little body in my arms and the intimate kisses of his tiny wet tongue on my hands worked their magic. I fell in love. For the past two years, I had lived in a world where brutality and violence ruled the streets, and where both people and pets disappeared or met cruel deaths, and here I suddenly held the warmth of new life and unconditional love in my very own arms. That walk home remained imprinted in my visceral memory for the rest of my life. It took an eternity, of course. My scrawny malnourished arms hurt and my legs were exhausted, so my mother offered several times to carry that little dog for me, but my dad would not allow her. I would only years later understand why not.

He insisted that I could do it, and reaching deep into my experience of loss and loneliness, he reminded me, "Remember it is hard for this little puppy also because we have just taken him away from his brothers and sisters, so he needs a lot of love and attention."

"He'll be lonely," I whispered.

"Not if he has you," my dad replied.

I hugged Beertje tighter and made it all the way home with him eventually falling asleep in my arms.

I have always been grateful for my father's wisdom and am convinced that this was one of the greatest gifts he ever gave me in those crucial weeks immediately after the war ended. On that long, long walk home, that little dog reawakened me to the love, pleasure, and warmth of mammalian touch, the sensuous pulse at the heart of life, and our immense human capacity to heal our own trauma by caring for another.

From that moment on, I rushed home from school each day to feed and take care of my new little friend. Beertje made me feel less alone, and he quickly became an indispensable part of our growing family. He must also have been important to my father, the amateur photographer, because Beertje would always appear prominently in family photographs of that challenging, postwar era. And one summer's evening out on our verandah, our little mutt, whose ancestry was clearly of a diverse variety, surprised us all with a full-throated howl at the full moon.

"Well, well, listen to him," my father said. "He's calling out to his ancestors."

"Just like a wolf," I added.

"It's the miracle of the moonlight in the dark," my mother whispered.

Then, not too many months later, my mother sat me down in the living room to tell me about some very big news. With a triumphant smile on her face, she put my hand on her rounded belly where it had stretched the fabric of her dress tight.

I almost immediately felt a little lump move inside of her and push against the palm of my hand as if it knew I was there.

"That is your little sister or brother." My mother laughed.

I told her that I really would like it to be a little sister, but assured her that it would be all right if it turned out to be a little brother. My mom said that was up to God, so before bedtime each night I began to send up prayers to this ever-present, mysterious God that He let it be a little sister, just in case. But I promised Beertje that I would not love her more than I loved him, even if it was a sister, and that since we had taken him away from his brothers and sisters, he could now share mine.

# Chapter 23

# Babies Everywhere!

The old city center of Amsterdam looked like a young girl dressed up for a birthday party on that particular morning the following spring. Blazing displays of spring flowers of every kind and color flowed from window boxes and planters that had been set out along the cobblestone streets and on bridges that spanned the numerous canals. Colorful flags and banners—the red, white, and blue of our nation; the royal orange for the monarchy; and the municipal black, red, and white ensigns of the city itself—flapped in a gentle breeze from windows along the canals, flagstaffs on buildings, and lampposts in the city squares. Even the weather, unusually warm for the month of May, supported its festive mood. One year exactly since the war had ended and our city had been liberated, and the citizens of Amsterdam were ready to party, but I also had an important personal reason to celebrate. Today my baby sister, Laura Margaretha, was coming home.

Born two weeks earlier, she and my mother had been held in the hospital for observation, since pregnancy and the process of giving birth still held possible complications for a woman who had been suffering from malnutrition and the aftereffects of starvation when she conceived. Nervous and worried, I now waited at my bedroom window for their arrival. I had bitten my nails down to the cuticles so they bled, even though my father—and even aunts and uncles I had not seen for years—told me not to worry so much.

"Your mom and baby sister are just fine. Now stop biting your nails," my dad had said, getting annoyed with me, as we both missed my mother.

But today was the day that my wish would come true, and while waiting, I filled the time by hopping up on a chair to look out the window and back down to the floor where Beertje, who had now grown into a lovable, medium-sized dog, sat at my feet and gave me an impatient little *woof, woof* as I talked to him about having to share attention with our new sister. Talking to our animals was always considered normal in our family, even for the adults; and yes, we talk to our plants also.

When the taxicab finally arrived, I watched my dad climb out first and stretch out his arm to steady my mother, who was holding a small bundle wrapped in pale blue bunting. I ran to the front door where, once inside, my mother unwrapped the bunting and placed a tiny little creature in my arms.

"She is so small," I whispered in extraordinary disbelief that this tiny being could survive.

"She is strong." My mom smiled. "She weighed more than eight pounds."

Not convinced, I could see this little baby was going to need a lot of protection, and I thought it was very wise of my parents to decide to place her crib in my room because, after all, I was her big sister. I would have to be strong for her. I could do that, I decided after a moment's hesitation at seeing how small and dependent she really was.

Over the next few weeks, my mother enlisted me in the caretaking of our new baby, and gradually my enhanced status as a big sister gave me increased confidence in my place in the world. So much so that I decided one day to confront my neighbor friend Maria and tell her that she had obviously been wrong when she had said that the reason I did not have a sister or brother was because God liked Catholics better than non-Catholics.

"You were wrong," I said, when I saw her go up the stairs that afternoon.

"About what?" she asked.

I told her that clearly it didn't make any difference to God if you were a Catholic or not, because I too now had a sister just like her. She looked baffled. It was evident that our theological conversation had not been of as great an importance to her as it had been to me.

"I never said that," she snarled. "Besides, I don't even want to be a Catholic anymore."

"Why not?" I asked somewhat naïvely, because I was not aware that one had a choice.

"Because I don't want all those babies." She grimaced. "My mom is having another baby. Even she doesn't want it. Sheesh, now I will have to share my bedroom with two sisters."

"But don't you like that? I really want to share my room with my little sister," I said in surprise.

"Yes, that's because you only have one." Maria sighed with exasperation at my naïveté. "No, I am going to be a nun."

My head swirled. "But don't you have to be a Catholic to be a nun?" I asked in confusion.

"I suppose so, but when I am a nun, I don't have to have all those babies. Everyone is having babies."

We sat down on the stairs together as I nodded in agreement. It did seem like there were suddenly babies everywhere. One of my aunts, whom everyone in my father's large family spoke of as "the spinster" and thought would be childless for the rest of her life, got married and just had a baby at the same time as my mom. School friends' mothers were expecting babies, and on the once-bleak streets of Amsterdam, pregnant women and mothers pushing baby carriages had suddenly sprung up like mushrooms after a long rain. On Wednesday afternoons when school was traditionally closed, I now accompanied my mother and aunt on their walks to the Vondelpark, the large central park in Amsterdam, where they took my little sister and niece for fresh air and playtime. I had to admit that I often felt out of place among all those gurgling and crying infants fussed over by doting, laughing mothers who seemed to have completely forgotten the dark and dangerous times of the past.

In an unexpected kinship, I agreed with Maria. "Yes, there are certainly a lot of them." And seated on those stairs between our apartments, we sighed in unison as if we were two burdened little old women instead of still children ourselves.

Maybe it was just the presence of all these new babies around us, but I was still trying to process the whole quandary of the God connection to the number of babies one had to have. As a girl, the question of God and motherhood confused and preoccupied me. My two grandmothers had eleven and seven children respectively, but my aunts had only two or three. I had been told by my mother that her mother had not wanted all those children, but had wanted to be a theologian and a writer. So why did she have all those babies anyway? As always, I decided to ask my mother, who could usually be depended on for a straightforward answer, even if she sometimes added too many facts for me to absorb.

"Mommy, Maria says if you are Catholic you have to have more babies. Is that true?" I asked her as she was bathing my little sister, Laura, in a small bathtub that she had put across two straight-backed chairs in the dining area of our living room.

My dad, always the rational agnostic, was reading the newspaper, and I heard him chortle.

My mother, looking a little shocked, replied carefully, "Well actually, I think this is something better discussed when you are older."

I was disappointed, because I was well aware of how babies were made—something no adult ever seemed to want to discuss either, even though among the kids at school it was a topic of infinite interest—but I really wanted an explanation for the Catholic and God thing. She saw my confusion and added, "Catholics have to listen to what their priest tells them. We Protestants can talk to God and decide for ourselves. But don't worry about it now. You will understand when you're older."

I started to argue, "But does God say something different to the priest . . . ?" "Enough now," my mom said wearily. I knew she was getting annoyed with me, but these God things that people threw around made my mind spin with perplexing questions that no one seemed to have answers to.

She shook her head and sighed. "You are just like my mother, always asking questions about religion."

When my mother compared me to her mother in that tone of voice, it never sounded like a compliment and always left me even more confused. I certainly did not want eleven babies, and why had my grandma not become the theologian or the writer she wished to be, anyway? Why had she given up on her own dreams? I wondered if maybe no one had answered her questions either.

At this point my dad put aside his newspaper, sat down opposite me, and said that different religions had laws and rules that were made by people, not by God. He added, "We are human beings and free to think for ourselves, but many people don't want to think for themselves. They would rather be told what to do."

Now, I was totally bewildered. "Why do people want to be told what to do?"

"It is easier. When you are free to make a choice, you also become responsible for it," my dad replied. "Sometimes that can be difficult.

Remember when I asked you to decide for yourself if you really wanted Beertje?"

Yes, I remembered. "I got very, very tired carrying him home. It was hard."

My dad added, "And when you got home?"

"I had to feed and brush him, and we still have to take him for his walks."

My dad smiled. "But it was your choice. You decided you wanted him. Some people don't want that responsibility. They want others, like priests or gods, to make the decisions for them."

My mother had finished bathing my sister and brought her to me to hold. She smelled sweet and fresh when I held her in my arms, and she made me smile when she grabbed my finger and squeezed it with her tiny hand.

I wanted to ask my dad more, but he had returned to reading his newspaper. The conversation had ended.

I decided that maybe my mother was right, and I should stop thinking about it until I was older, but just in case, I told God before I went to sleep that night that I would probably like four children, two boys and two girls, when I got married one day. That way each would have a playmate, but no more than four. I thanked Him again for giving me a baby sister, although I was beginning to suspect that it had more to do with my father than God, but I thought God would like to be thanked anyway, and it would make my mother happy.

That night I drifted asleep on the thought that all the priests in the world must be very happy because of all the babies being born. I was too young to be aware yet of the impact that our exploding population would have on Holland's postwar economy and eventually on my family's destiny.

# Chapter 24

# Postwar Shadows

"To the future!" The family members gathered in our living room raised their glasses in an optimistic toast as they took turns holding my new baby sister in their laps.

"Yes, here is to the future!" my parents echoed.

Of late our home had filled up with visitors: aunts, uncles, and cousins whom I had not seen for many years. Having survived their own personal wartime traumas, they now came to celebrate the newest baby in the extended family. Our damp little country had persevered through the horrors of a world gone mad, and friends and family who gathered in our living room agreed, "It's best not to talk about the past, best to forget what happened and get on with life. To the future!" My chubby, postwar baby sister with her sweet smile, large cornflower-blue eyes, and wisps of blond, silky hair, who was now being passed around from arm to arm, looked every bit the picture postcard image of the healthy little Dutch girl who symbolized for all the new life they longed for in the years ahead.

But despite the good intentions and hopeful celebrations, the shadows of the war would continue to haunt us like ghosts that refused to be put to rest. Something was not right with my parents. Something had never been totally right with my dad since he'd returned from Germany, and it seemed to be getting worse. In the middle of the night, I woke to hear him roaming through the rooms of our small urban apartment, and as he stumbled and swore in his deep guttural voice, I knew that he was desperately searching for a cigarette. If he could not find one, he undid the old butts in the ashtrays and even those he had tossed on the living room floor as if he were still in the camp, if my mother hadn't picked them up yet. Even in the dark, his fingers could roll the half-burnt tobacco remnants into the thin slips of paper with which he shaped them into the magical cigarette that delivered the necessary nicotine to appease his demons, at least for a few minutes.

On some afternoons after school, I helped him with the rolling of the tobacco in the hope that if he smoked more cigarettes he would not be so sad or angry. He always smiled and thanked me.

He would tell me many years later that he struggled with a double sense of betrayal in those days. While his ancestral roots, both on his mother's and father's sides, reached back centuries deep into the Friesian soil of the Netherlands, my dad had been born in Cologne, Germany. He had lived there until he was seven years old, when his father was killed in a tragic accident in the shipyard where he had worked. Having been raised and attended school in Germany, my father was fluent in both Dutch and German, and like many first-generation children born in foreign lands, he felt a link with two nations, the nation of his parents and ancestors and the country of his birth.

As an adult he could read the great literature of Goethe and Schiller in the original German but struggled to understand the German people and culture's embrace of Hitler's message of hatred and prejudice.

He refused to talk about the experience of his incarceration in the camp, but sometimes in one of his darker moods he let it slip that he "had to dig graves," and revealed that he had attempted to escape on two occasions, once after seeing his friend being "blown up by a grenade."

But if my mother or I asked him to say more about his experiences, he replied that "a man" did not speak about those things, because men of his generation were raised in a gender-biased culture that expected them to suppress their memories and feelings.

Only once, when a conversation with his brother turned to politics and communism, did I hear my father draw on his memories to make a point as he raged at witnessing "Slavic prisoners, stripped naked and pinned to barbed wire in the midst of winter while Nazi camp commandants sprayed them with icy cold water from hoses till they died."

I listened in horror until my father, noticing my rapt attention, suddenly went silent. "*Ach.* Damn it!" He shook his head. "What's the use? Let's stop talking." He attempted a forced smile, and I could feel the warmth in his trying, but the deep fatigue in his voice and face could not quite catch up as he lit yet another cigarette from the one still between his lips. He then invited his brother to "go for a beer," while I stayed home with my mother and sister.

I would learn many years later about Post Traumatic Stress Disorder, but at the time, my mother and I knew only that the man who had returned from the POW camp was not the same calm, steady, storytelling dad I had known. The dad who'd returned increasingly flew into unexpected rages or disappeared into long withdrawn silences.

Friends and family who visited us admonished him with reminders: "Hein, you must count your blessings. Your family survived."

But neither his family nor his beloved Amsterdam could restore his broken trust in humanity. He admitted to feeling "suffocated" in the narrowness of the cobblestoned streets. "It's not the same city, just not the same," he would repeat, mostly talking to himself.

The Dutch economy was in shambles, and like many other men in those immediate postwar years in Holland, my father had trouble finding suitable work. He had always shown an entrepreneurial spirit and enjoyed creating things with his own hands. Before his incarceration in Germany, he had established a small but growing manufacturing business in rubber goods. It gave him the satisfaction of being the strong male provider he wanted to be for his wife and family. But when he returned from Germany, he learned like so many other small business owners that the Nazis had confiscated his inventory and equipment, and the lease on the building had permanently expired. Many of the men with whom he had done business were Jewish and never came home.

Worries about our financial security dominated the conversations between my parents that I could not help but overhear.

"What should we do?" my mother asked frequently.

"We will manage," my father insisted.

My mother struggled with her own ghosts. She hoarded cans of food in cupboards that were locked to us, reserved "in case there is another famine."

She also tried with great determination to discover which of our neighbors had betrayed us and had leaked the secret of our hiding Nel to the Nazi collaborators. She shared suspicions with me that could not be proven, and, in her obsessive quest, my mother too could not find a way to heal her damaged sense of trust in her fellow human beings.

When the war ended, a significant number of well-known collaborators were caught and punished. Many received the death sentence, but others escaped with minor sentences or no punishment at all. And, in a need to express their helpless rage and pain, ordinary citizens who had been starved and humiliated took a stance of moral righteousness that often went to its own extremes. Children of collaborators were shunned and shamed for their parents' acts of betrayal, and young girls suspected of having befriended German soldiers, sometimes for food and survival or simply out of romantic young ignorance, had their heads shaven and were put on public display as in medieval witch-hunts. The long war with its Nazi occupation of our city had destroyed the bonds of human trust. They would take a long time to heal.

"I think it would help if we moved to another part of the city where I don't have those memories," my mother told my father and me, and she began to concentrate her energy on finding a new place to live. She scoured the different neighborhoods for possibilities and, excited by every prospect, rushed out each day to check them out, often dragging me along with her.

"I have a hunch this one may work out, and I want to make sure you like it," she would say with an excitement that she hoped I would catch. But each and every search just led to another disappointment. Someone else had grabbed the flat first, or, after endless hours of walking, my mother would discover that its availability proved to be just another rumor, and the flat didn't exist in the first place.

I found myself getting annoyed with her repeated attempts and the pressure I felt to join her in her ramped-up excitement, and I experienced a sense of guilty relief when, after months of searching, it became painfully apparent that a move would probably prove unfeasible.

With the return of the men, young couples wanting to marry and move out on their own, and the explosive number of babies being born, a severe housing shortage in Amsterdam had made a move not only difficult but virtually impossible. No new housing had been constructed during the war years, while existing houses had deteriorated through wear and tear, sometimes gutted by those who used the wood to keep warm in their attempt to survive the deadly Hunger Winter. As a result, multiple generations were already crowding together in confined spaces, and apartment exchanges had become part of a new postwar black market in which large sums of money changed hands, and flats secretly went to the highest bidder. Sadly, it was rumored that those who had stood by and done nothing—or worse—during the occupation were often able to outbid those who suffered or risked their lives for their country.

Never one to give up easily, my mother voiced her frustrations with increased rancor and continued to sift through the newspapers each day, while my father withdrew and lit yet another cigarette as he tried to figure out new ways to make a living.

"To the future," they toasted optimistically with friends and family, but the ghosts of war continued to haunt our home.

# Chapter 25

# A Family in Transition

"I want you to come for a walk with me," my mother greeted me, a serious expression on her face, when I came out of the school building after class one particular afternoon.

"Mommy, what's wrong?" I was worried.

My mother never came to pick me up from school anymore, so what was she doing here waiting for me?

"Mr. Sleumer is dead," she said. "He died of a heart attack. I just heard."

"Oh, I am so sorry." I saw that she had tears in her eyes, which made me feel uncomfortable for some reason I could not yet determine. "I am sorry," I repeated. "You liked him."

"Yes," my mother said, "he was a good man."

The two of us walked along the canal in silence for a while and then sat down on the smooth, hollowed-out stone steps that fronted one of the old seventeenth-century buildings that had once been a proud burgher's family home, but now housed only the impersonal offices of some unknown business.

"It's strange to think of him gone," my mother said as she stared ahead at the other side of the canal.

I nodded in agreement. For a moment, I thought of Mr. Sleumer standing at the top of the garden steps, my mother disheveled on the ground as she hacked away at the radios. Such a long time ago it seemed, and I shook off the image. I would rather remember his kindness and enthusiasm when he brought me a new cigar band or an exotic stamp from a country I had not yet heard of.

"It was nice of him to bring me cigar bands and stamps. I always liked that," I told her.

"He even helped you paste them into albums and locate countries on the map," my mother said.

"Yes," I agreed and then added, "but he could never be Daddy."

My mother looked a little surprised and said, "Well, of course not, and you made it very clear that you did not want him to try." Then she smiled. "Remember how you wouldn't even let him hug you when we were all at Mia's place?"

I did remember. "I didn't want him to think he could be Daddy."

"No, he was not Daddy, but he was a good man," my mother repeated softly.

She took my hand and we sat on those stone steps reminiscing about a time only she and I knew.

"He told me to be a good girl for you," I said. "He loved you, didn't he?"

"Oh, Henny." My mother's voice sank to a whisper. "It was war. We shared a goal to fight oppression, to fight for freedom. We both believed in the underground."

Then she added, "He was in love with a woman in France, you know."

I had not known that and asked, "What happened?"

My mother shrugged her shoulders. "The war happened."

She stood up and brushed her skirt down.

"I'm not sure if I will tell Daddy," she said.

I knew that my parents' relationship had been under stress. Both were avid conversationalists, but of late their communication had escalated into arguments. I understood in later years that my mother considered their marriage too fragile to openly grieve the loss of another man, especially a man with whom she had so deeply shared the darkest, most intense moments of her life.

The war with its two-year separation had changed both my parents. Each carried traumatic memories that could not be soothed by the other, and this created an emotional distance. My father responded with impatience and long periods of silent withdrawal behind his newspaper to my mother's outbursts of frustration at the impossibility of finding a new home in a different neighborhood away from her memories. In turn, his mood swings triggered my mother's angry, tearful anxiety. Their relationship hung suspended over a two-year deep chasm of separate trauma and experiences that shattered the culturally prescribed gender roles that had once given them the solid ground from which to proceed.

My mother was not the same adoring woman who looked up to her husband for support and safety, and my father was no longer the calm, confident man she married. Before he left, my father, like most men of his generation, felt secure in his role as the protector and provider of his family. Culture had bestowed upon him a place in the scheme of things that went unquestioned and unexamined. He was the undisputed head of the family, our hero who went out into the world to slay the dragons of work, money, and other dangers that lurked outside the protective walls of our home. One day in the future, when I was involved in my own identity struggles, he would admit to me that he had experienced a certain security in that role despite its drawbacks, drawbacks that were not acknowledged, of course, because men of his generation were not encouraged to talk about their feelings.

But the war had broken down those carefully constructed roles and walls. Women and men worked side by side in their resistance to the Nazi oppression, and while my father had been forced into slave labor, my mother had experienced the respect of other men in her role as a fellow fighter for freedom in the underground.

Having been unable to protect his wife and child from the horrors of the war, my father now found it unbearable that he could not solve and fix our postwar challenges. He and my mother got lost in an emotional maze when they attempted to talk with each other about their hopes for the future and experiences of the past.

In the days after Mr. Sleumer's death, my parents' disagreements escalated. And while they kept their quarrels mostly confined behind the closed door of their bedroom, so that I could not make out their words even when I stood near the door to listen, I worried because I could hear the sound of my mother's tearful crying and the anger in my father's voice.

Then one Saturday afternoon, they stayed in their bedroom arguing longer than ever before. I had been reading in my own room and wondered when they were finally going to be done, when I suddenly heard my father's loud yell: "Enough! I am leaving! I have to get out of here!" With his words echoing in the hallway, he slammed the bedroom door behind him and strode toward the front door.

I catapulted to my feet and stormed ahead of him. With an explosive burst of total panic, I managed to reach the door first. Spreading my arms wide to block his exit, I looked up at him and screamed from a deep, desperate part of myself: "No, no, no, you cannot leave! I won't let you! No! No!"

My father stood still and stared down at me with a shocked expression on his face. Then, as if in slow motion, he turned around and walked into the main room where he sat down at the dining table with his head in his hands. He looked at me and shook his head. "It's all right. I am not going anywhere. *Ach*, sometimes people say stupid things they don't mean."

I couldn't speak and tried to blink away the tears in my eyes as he pulled me toward him. "Sometimes husbands and wives fight and say hurtful things to each other. Don't take it too seriously. We will figure it out. I am not leaving. I promise you." He put his arm around me and hugged me tight. "I promise you."

I would never totally understand the why or the how of it, but in that moment I believed him with every intuitive fiber in my body. He pulled out a chair for me, and I sat close to him at the table.

"I'll make us some tea," my mother said, her calm voice reflecting the quiet that had settled over the room.

The kettle boiled, my mother made a pot of tea, placed the pot and cups on the dining room table, walked into my bedroom to pick up my little sister who had woken up from her nap, and we gathered around the dining room table as we sipped our tea and talked baby talk to my little sister that made her laugh. We were a family in transition.

In the years ahead I would maintain a belief that my intervention of tears and screams of "No, no, no!" while blocking the front door with my arms widespread had shocked my parents into sanity and saved their marriage. My grandiose conviction was probably unfounded, but it helped ward off the devastating fear of another abandonment that I possibly could not have handled emotionally on the heels of the war. Traumatized children are known to take responsibility for events over which they had little or no control.

I would remember that the death of Mr. Sleumer and my father's threatening to leave sparked a turning point in my parents' marriage. As I lay in my bed in the evenings, I could hear them talking late into the night about other marriages of friends and family that had not survived the trauma and long separations of the war, and it reassured me to hear them tell each other that they were going to make theirs work.

One afternoon after the explosive event, my mother shared with me that she and my dad had reached an agreement acceptable to both of them that they would never again discuss the experiences each had suffered during those two years apart from each other.

"It's better that way," she explained to me. "We each did the best we could. It was war. We survived it. That's what's important. We must focus on our family now."

My father approached the course correction in their marriage in his own unique way. "We need to stop talking and start doing more things together," he said at the dinner table one evening and, turning to me, added, "You need to learn to ride a bike." It was true that I had never learned to ride a bike during the years of the war and its aftermath. My father laughed and said, "You can't be a Dutch girl and not ride a bike."

In the following weeks, he acquired two old bicycles that he restored for himself and for me, his with a special seat in the front for my little sister. He then asked me to come along to help him choose the brand-new bicycle he planned to purchase for my mother. "She is your mother," he said. "She should have a new bicycle."

I agreed. His love and respect for her made me feel safe and secure. After all, I planned to be a mother myself one day.

It did not take me long to learn to ride my bike as my parents and neighbors cheered me on in the street in front of our home. Soon our little family of four began to take regular, long weekend bike rides in the countryside, where I could see my father relax and breathe a little easier, even as my mother fussed that she had not really needed such an expensive new bicycle. Often on Sundays my mother packed us a picnic lunch. We would ride our bicycles to a large park, Het Bos, outside the city and there, seated on the grass, our bicycles leaning against an old white birch tree, my parents relaxed and shared thoughts and plans for the future. I usually read one of the many books I regularly devoured, and my increasingly adventurous little sister demanded the attention of all three of us with her newly acquired habit of wandering away to explore the various bugs that she spotted on the trees and in the grass.

On one such outing my mother admitted to us that she still had not totally accepted that we would be unable to find another place to live in Amsterdam.

"I guess I will always dream about finding a place to live where I can feel at peace," she said.

My father nodded and said, "I understand." He shared that he too, at times, dreamed about wide-open spaces of land and new opportunities away from the memories of our city and the war.

He philosophized, "*Ach*, the human spirit yearns to be free."

I interrupted to remind him, "Daddy, the war is over. We are free now."

He just smiled and replied, "A person's spirit can feel imprisoned, even when the body seems to be free," but he did not articulate the freedom he yearned for. However, I noticed that my mother smiled and nodded in apparent agreement.

Men of my father's generation were not given the luxury of expressing their deep feelings, but my parents appeared to have reached a sense of peace with each other that was expressed in their open philosophical meanderings and a newly acquired camaraderie that brought a new lightness to our home and made me feel relaxed in their presence. In the evenings, while I did my homework and my little sister, Laura, slept peacefully, they played a regular game of chess that my mother frequently won. My father read, my mother knitted, they went to a movie or socialized with family and friends, and sometimes late at night, I woke up to sighs and exclamations of lovemaking. I thought my world was finally secure.

# Chapter 26

# The Death of a Mother

Sometimes fate gives destiny an unexpected push. I knew the moment my mother walked into the classroom that something serious had happened, even before she and my teacher exchanged a few words in low voices and he motioned me with his hand to come to the front of the class.

"You need to pack your things and go home with your mother," he said, adding, "I am sorry, it's your grandmother."

I followed my mother out of the school building as she shared with me that my beloved "little grandma," my Omaatje, had suffered a massive stroke and was not expected to live.

"I thought you'd like to come with me to Rotterdam to say good-bye to her," my mom said. She added that my father would stay in Amsterdam to take care of my little sister.

My feelings did a confusing two-step back-and-forth from sadness about losing my grandma to pleasure at the thought of seeing my favorite cousins, Netty and Loura, with whom we were to stay in Rotterdam. Of course, I was still blissfully unaware of the family dynamic that once again aligned my mother and me with the past, a separate unit from my father and little sister. But there we were, a couple of hours later, just the two of us on that familiar train ride to Rotterdam.

I could not imagine my Omaatje being gone. She had visited us not too long ago. I had just begun to study French at school, and she had lavished me with praise when she attended the play that my French class put on in which I stepped out of a life-size cardboard box onto the stage and announced my one speaking line in my very best French: "Je suis une poupée." (I am a doll.) She had shared with me that she too had studied French as a young girl and had even visited Paris with her parents. She had wanted to write stories and study theology—questions about God and religion, she explained. But that was before she got married, had eleven children, and lost her own dreams.

Grandma died peacefully soon after we arrived, and my mother and I were swallowed up in the family gatherings where grandma's nine surviving children, their spouses, and numerous grandchildren shared their grief, memories, and anecdotes about their mother. We young ones were relegated to other rooms to spend time with our cousins, especially after a family argument broke out between my mother and one of her brothers about her involvement in the resistance during the war and the fact that she had risked the life of her own child by hiding a Jewish girl in our home.

He clearly disapproved and questioned her in a belligerent voice: "What possessed you to put the life of your own child in danger?"

My mother replied, "Because I would hope someone would do the same for her if circumstances were the other way around."

"Oh," my uncle snickered, "you always were a foolish idealist."

But with that penetrating glance that I had come to know so well from the intense years we had shared during the war, she stood her ground and said, "Yes, foolish, because I want my children to grow up in a more just world."

My uncle raised his voice: "Such a world won't ever happen. You are a mother. A mother! Your responsibility was the safety of your own child!"

The room grew silent, and I could barely breathe as she answered him: "But don't you understand that is exactly why I did it," and pointing her finger at his chest as if in reprimand, she added, "Don't you realize that not one of our children is safe unless they are all safe."

"Oh that's just stupid, foolish nonsense," he scoffed. At which point other family members chimed in to defend my mother, and one of my aunts shooed us children out of the room and out of earshot of the ensuing argument.

But something new broke into my awareness during that exchange between my mother and my uncle that would continue to plague me well into my adult years. In that crucial moment, a moment that would etch itself on my memory, I heard as if for the very first time how carelessly the word *foolish* rolled off men's lips and how acceptable it seemed to them to address my mother in a tone of voice that belittled her as if she were a small, ignorant child. Memories of the Dutch Nazis mocking her for hiding "the Jewess" and the Amsterdam bureaucrat's condescension as he lectured her on losing her identity card that had been stolen merged with the dismissive tone of my uncle's scorn. I knew for certain in that moment that no one, absolutely no one, would have spoken to my father in that demeaning way, and it awakened a feeling of anger in me at an injustice I could not yet clearly name.

It was probably not surprising that in a family of so many siblings and all their spouses and significant others, political and emotional values would span a wide range. The history of those who actively risked their own lives and those of their families to resist the Nazis in the Netherlands during the war was uneven, and with their mother's death, sibling disagreements and ideological differences emerged and, perhaps in the heat of grief, were finding their voice in individual expression. Grandma was a strong woman who had given birth to eleven children and raised seven sons and three daughters to adulthood. She had been the magnet around which the family had always gathered.

"Your grandmother held a center in the family that has now gone," my mother whispered when a couple of days later she and I once again rode the train back to Amsterdam, just the two of us. We held each other's hand and shared the embroidered lace handkerchief that had once belonged to my grandmother to wipe the tears from our eyes. I felt my mother's sadness, as I always did, but I could also feel my own excitement to be going home again to my dad and my little sister and our own little family.

As the train continued to rumble toward Amsterdam, I said to my mother, "I don't think your brother should have called you 'foolish' or 'stupid.'"

My mother looked surprised and then, shrugging her shoulders in that way of hers, said, "He had just lost his mother."

"I still don't think he should have said that," I argued.

"Yes, but I did put our lives—and your life—in danger," my mother said softly and looked away. Then she turned to face me and declared in a voice strong with conviction, "But I could not just sit by and do nothing. I just could not. It would have been wrong."

"You helped save Nel's life," I said, "and I am really happy you did."

"Her life should never have been in danger in the first place, that's the whole point," my mother replied. She placed a hand over the back of my hand and commanded, "You must always fight against oppression. Always fight for freedom. Always!"

Freedom was the principle my mother would always tell me she valued most. Even years later when, as a young woman, I would talk to her of such values as "love and empathy," her answer would be, "give me peace and freedom." But on that train ride back to our home in Amsterdam, I could not yet anticipate how her mother's death had just given her the ultimate freedom to leave the past behind and change the trajectory of our lives.

The war had been over for several years, but its cruelties had left a mark on a generation of families and continued to traumatize the Dutch culture. The deep healing of the wounds would take many more years and manifest in different ways for each family and individual.

For many people, the postwar politics of conflicting values among those in power did not create the "better society" that Queen Wilhelmina and many resistance workers had hoped for. The Dutch economy would continue to flounder in the years ahead, as our ravaged little country and its citizens struggled with massive under- and unemployment as well as severe housing shortages for a rapidly growing population.

Ultimately, the values that proved of most importance to my parents would shape the course of my destiny, but on the train at that moment, I just looked forward to going home to be with my dad and my little sister again. I missed them and felt sad that my grandma could no longer grow the geraniums she had loved. I wished that she had written the stories she'd longed to write so that I could read them now.

# Chapter 27

# "The End of an Era . . ."

**M**y dad had bought six thick bars of dark chocolate and my mother's favorite assortment of mums that he'd arranged in a large crystal vase on the dining room table to celebrate our homecoming from grandma's funeral.

"We missed you," he said, as he carried my little sister around on his shoulders while calling her by the funny little nickname that he had coined for her with great mirth. In his sharing of it with me, he thought it would make me laugh also, because he had taken it out of one of my favorite stories about two kindly giants, a pompous little king, and a tiny court jester, a story my father and I shared when I was the one who sat on his lap. Once I could never hear enough of the antics of the two bulky giants, especially when my father mimicked their friendly teasing of the gullible court jester, but now all it did was make me painfully aware that I was no longer his little girl. These days that role belonged to the sweet, smiling, blonde cherub who clapped her little hands as she basked in her daddy's attention.

The tentacles of war were not done with me yet. Although my sleepwalking episodes had ended and I no longer felt the need to steal food out of cupboards or stores, I suffered from a chronic hacking cough for which the doctors could find no cause, and I had a nervous habit of biting my nails down to the cuticles until they bled, causing my mother to constantly worry about me.

"War nerves," the doctor had told my parents. He had seen the symptoms in other children and could offer no cure except time.

I was the "damaged" child. When relatives and friends visited to celebrate the new life of my sister and the other postwar babies being born to family members, and everyone toasted with exuberance to the future, I often felt in an odd way like I did not belong. Being the old, dark child of the past, I was the one bound to my mother through the secret memories that everyone wanted to leave behind and forget. I did not want to be that girl, but the only way I could escape her sadness, her anger, and a longing that had no words was to lose myself, either in the books on every topic that I devoured from the local library, or in the swimming pool where I could feel the strength of my own young body.

My mother had been a competitive runner and national speed walking champion in her unmarried days. She firmly believed that sport was not just necessary for a healthy body but that it built character, so from my earliest years she encouraged—actually forced— me to run also. To her chagrin and disappointment, however, I had a tendency to trip, stumble, and sprain my ankles, and I really did not enjoy running. At her insistence I had enrolled in a few neighborhood competitions, but watching her daughter "trip, fall, and make a fool of herself and her mother," as she unsympathetically quipped, she became finally convinced that I was not meant to be a runner. Never one to miss changing a problem into a challenge to be overcome, she then decided that I must be more like my father and enrolled me in a swim club instead.

My father had indeed been a strong swimmer who took a job as an usher in the 1928 Olympic Games held in Amsterdam just so he could watch Johnny Weissmuller swim. Weissmuller, swimming's first superstar, won two gold medals in those Games and my dad relished telling the story about being right there to watch and cheer on his hero, the champion swimmer who would eventually become the vine-swinging Tarzan of Hollywood movies.

Fortunately, the narrow ankles and slightly splayed toes that made my feet look a little like ducks' feet and caused me to trip on land were a natural gift in the water. Once I entered the pool, my body felt as if it had come home. Within a short time of learning to swim, I was competing and winning junior races in breaststroke, and eventually also in butterfly and the individual medley. The pool at the YWCA where the ADZ (Amsterdam Ladies Swim Club) met became my second home. I loved absolutely everything about swimming: the camaraderie of the club members, the thrill of the race, even the smell of the chlorine, and especially the sensuality of feeling my body's own strength as it moved with ease and pleasure through the water. Swimming became my lifelong meditation.

But my mother also liked to swim, and the club that I belonged to was located in the YWCA, which offered a weekly evening mother-daughter swim. My mother insisted that it would be a fun thing for the two of us to do together, and I could not tell her that I preferred to swim with my friends or spend the evening at home with my dad and sister. It was my mother who regularly came to watch my practice swims, and it was she who stood up in the stands to cheer me as loudly as she could when I won my first competition in the twenty-five-meter breaststroke race, while my father stayed home with my little sister. But I remember how I wished that he too could have been there to see me win my very first race.

Then one day he came home with an armload of photographic equipment. It included a secondhand photographic enlarger, photo-sensitive paper, and trays for the alchemical baths that would turn the tiny 35 mm negatives from the camera that I had learned to load and unload when I was still his little girl into large photos suitable for framing.

"You and I are going to develop pictures," my father said to me, as I eyed his purchases with great curiosity, and he proceeded to enlist my help in transforming the kitchen into a photographic darkroom complete with a red lightbulb.

From that moment on, one night a week or sometimes on the weekend, he and I hijacked my mother's kitchen. Normally filled with the smells and tastes of my favorite meatballs and the cinnamon-flavored apple tarts filled with juicy apples and plump raisins that only my mother knew how to make, the kitchen became the place where my dad and I bonded. We covered the windows with dark blinds, cleared the countertops, filled trays with wicked chemical solutions, and turned that kitchen into a magic cave of image and light. There the two of us watched in excitement as barely visible images from tiny negatives slowly appeared as large clear photographs on the blank paper immersed in its mysterious baths, mostly photographs of family members and, of course, our faithful dog, Beertje.

In that darkroom, focused on the magic and alchemy of the photographic process, I came to accept that I would never be my daddy's little girl anymore. That role now belonged to Laura, my sweet, happy little sister who curled up with me in my bed in the mornings before I went to school and who asked me for stories at night. But my father and I began to form a new kind of relationship that loosened the tight trauma bond I had formed with my mother and made me feel less chained to the dark memories of the past. Gradually my chronic cough disappeared.

I still struggled with my questions about God at that time, but eventually would find a mentor in my sixth-grade teacher, Miss J. H. de Wilde, who urged my father to let me sit for the entrance examination to a lyceum in the south of Amsterdam that offered a curriculum in philosophy, religion, and literature. When my dad explained that he did not have the financial wherewithal to pay for me to attend a private Christian lyceum, even if I passed the exam, she encouraged him to apply for a merit scholarship. With the help of her tutoring, I both passed the exam and was accepted to the lyceum under a scholarship.

In the mentoring process that she undertook, Miss de Wilde, a deeply devout Christian woman, invited me to the home she shared with her sister and introduced me to their expansive library of books on other cultures. Miss de Wilde wisely replied to my questions about the various religious ritual practices and beliefs in the books I read by telling me not to worry too much because God was "a great and gentle listener," and she was certain that in time I would discover the answers I needed.

Around that time, the thought came to me that God need not be a father up in the clouds or in a heaven somewhere, but could be a great spirit that floated in and around the world, accessible if we needed help sorting things out. I then also decided that I was the reincarnation of a Peruvian princess. I don't know exactly how those conclusions came to me, but both suited me just fine.

Paradoxically, as the rich mystery of the universe expanded in my imagination, I began to spend less time in my inner conundrums and more time in the external reality, which had now become a safer and more inviting place. In the evening hours when my mother was busy with her knitting or the paper patterns from which she made our dresses, with my little sister asleep or playing with Beertje, my father oversaw my homework. He could be stern and expected me to be "smart." Any homework that appeared "sloppy" or not thought through would be torn up for me to do over again, and he would say, "This time, do it with careful attention."

But with his knowledge of four languages, his love of mythology, and a gift for showing me how culture influences language, he made my courses in Dutch, French, and English interesting and fun, and in the process we rediscovered our old shared delight in mythological stories, as we spotted heroes, tricksters, and serendipitous fate in all my assignments.

With the intent of creating financial stability for our family, my dad decided to learn the art and craft of making mirrors so that he could partner with his older brother, a master silverer, in a small business. Their workshop was located within walking distance of our home, and sometimes my mother, little sister, and I brought them lunch. When my father showed us how he turned clear glass into mirrors, I felt as I did when we looked at the emerging images in our photographic darkroom, that I was the daughter of a magician. I did not notice yet that my father's fingers that held his constant cigarette were now coated by the heavy metals in which a silverer worked. We would only learn many years later of the lethal connection and hidden consequences. But then, so much remains hidden behind the hope, hard work, and new beginnings that follow a war.

That was the year that our beloved Queen Wilhelmina announced her plans to abdicate her throne and transfer the reins of our country to her daughter, Juliana. On the day of the historic event in September of 1948, my parents took us to the Palace Square, where we stood near the same spot from which my mother and I had once run for our lives to escape the German snipers who had changed the celebration of our city's liberation into a bloodbath. I tucked the memory away in the corner of my mind that belonged to just my mother and me. Best to forget it and celebrate the four of us present now: my father, my mother, my sister, and me. We waited expectantly in front of the Royal Palace and when, at the stroke of noon, the old Queen Wilhelmina and the new Queen Juliana appeared on the balcony, I waved my orange flag and cheered with my parents and the rest of the crowd with joyous abandonment. We were safe.

Despite Hitler's attempt to destroy human freedom, our family had survived, and the Dutch monarchy remained intact, but

Wilhelmina's abdication "marked the end of an era," my father remarked sadly that day. I would soon discover that his words conveyed his mourning for the country that could no longer nourish his soul or provide a future for his family.

# Chapter 28

# Veterans of War

"**D**on't they ever go home?" I growled at my mother as I walked into our apartment after having been on a long bike ride with my friends. I joined her in opening the verandah doors of our living room to let in some fresh air. Wreathed in a haze of cigarette smoke that hung over the room like a shroud, my father's former military buddies had gathered at our home, like a company of ghosts rejoined after years of separate wandering, to share their rage and vent their frustrations with the Dutch government.

"It's a bloody insult when your own country tells you that you should leave if you want to have a future." I recognized the voice of Willem.

The war had been over for more than three years, but the Dutch economy was still in shambles, and the country continued to suffer from massive unemployment and a severe housing shortage for a growing population. In a desperate effort to solve its insurmountable problems, the Dutch government, with the support of its monarchy and both Protestant and Catholic churches, had made a historic decision to actively encourage young men and their families to emigrate if they wanted to secure a future for themselves.

Feeling betrayed by the country they had once served, the men in our living room had not been able to find jobs to match their skills or places to live for their new or growing young families. They had first met when Hitler rounded up former Dutch military, registered them as prisoners of war, and forced them to serve in German labor camps. Willem had ignored Hitler's order at the time and was dragged out of his home at gunpoint. Another man, named Geert, had gone into hiding but was discovered and beaten severely before being transported to Germany. In the years away from home, they had all experienced traumas they could not talk about. In the safety of my mother's living room, they drank their coffee, smoked their endless cigarettes, and expressed their anger.

I escaped to my bedroom where the air was clean and my three-year-old sister was just waking up from her nap. I picked her up when she reached out her hands and, with her usual sweet smile, pointed to the book from which she liked me to tell her a story. I loved the feel of my little sister on my lap and felt happy as she named the animals and objects in her picture book. My school studies were going well. I was competing and sometimes winning swim races and had been told by the coach of our team that I might have a chance at becoming a champion. I liked to hang out with my girlfriends, and the other day the popular blue-eyed boy a year my senior smiled at me in front of the school building and turned my knees so wobbly that I almost fell off my bike. Yes, I liked my life. My future self beckoned and made me impatient with my parents' old war issues and the political frustrations of the men in our living room, but I could not totally escape the conversations.

My mother called me to say she was serving coffee and pastries and needed my help, so my little sister and I walked back through the living room, in which the smoky air had been cleared and the rich smell of coffee created a friendlier atmosphere. We entered the kitchen where I was supposed to grind more fresh coffee from the little grinder that was attached to the wall next to the kitchen door that opened onto the back verandah. It was the door that had been kicked in by the Nazis who had once threatened our lives. It seemed like a long time ago. Now Beertje had his dog bed between the door and the kitchen stove, and Laura cuddled up to him while I stroked his furry head with one hand and turned the handle on the coffee grinder with the other.

"Pay attention to what you are doing," my mother said.

I handed her the glass container filled with freshly ground coffee. There really was no better smell than fresh coffee or hot chocolate, and I could already taste the sweetness of the tiny chocolate éclair that I spied on the pastry platter on the kitchen counter. As always, my mom warned me that I could only have the éclair if no one else took it but then relented, and with a smile she put it on a separate plate for me while handing me the tray with coffee cups to take to the men.

"You are growing up to become a little beauty." Willem grinned at me as I handed him his coffee cup. I could feel my cheeks go hot and knew my face was turning red. Darn him. I didn't quite know what to do with my feelings that in equal measure both liked and hated his male admiration.

A tall, young man with an easy manner and a crooked smile, Willem sometimes seemed closer to my age than my parents'. Dark-haired with a Mediterranean complexion, he had amazing green eyes that I noticed because he sometimes winked at me when my dad and mom weren't looking.

Like my dad, he was never without a cigarette in his hand, and my mom had remarked that, "Willem likes his beer a little too much."

Even though he had told my father that he always thought of himself as a confirmed bachelor, he had found a girl he wanted to marry. But how could he think of starting his own family if he could not find a decent place for them to live?

My parents sympathized with Willem. The postwar lack of available housing had impacted many families, including our own. Even though my mother assured us she had accepted the reality that in the foreseeable future we would not be able to move away from our current home with its wartime memories, she still from time to time followed up on rumors of someone wanting to exchange or rent out their apartment, only to be disappointed once again. And my older cousin, the daughter of my father's brother and business partner, had been waiting to get married for a long time, but like so many other couples, she and her fiancé had not been able to find a place of their own to live. Finally, after endless searching, they joined countless other young couples who saw no other option but to move into cramped living quarters with their parents. Young and old were trying to make the best of it, but the lack of housing intensified the stresses brought on by a flagging economy, especially for small business owners like my dad and uncle who could barely make ends meet.

"Maybe we should just tell the bastard government here to lump it and move to Australia or Canada. I've been told they have huge open spaces of land where you can build your own house," Willem exclaimed. Then appealing to my dad's love of horses and their service in the Dutch cavalry, he added with a grin, "Hey, Hein, we could even get ourselves some horses."

"You are not really suggesting we leave Holland," said my mother, walking in from the kitchen and interrupting the male fantasy. "And in my home, watch your language."

Willem looked up at her. "Sorry, Miep, but wouldn't you like to have a house of your own with land around it? A new fresh start?"

I watched my dad gaze at my mother and speak the words I imagined she was thinking: "To leave our families behind. That would be a very hard decision."

Willem replied in a sharp tone, "Your parents are all dead. No mothers, no fathers to hold you here. You are talking about your brothers and sisters, but what about her," he asked, pointing at me, "and the little one? Can you see a future here for them?"

My mother started to say something, but Willem interrupted and turned his head in my direction. "You know, when she is ready to get married and start her own family, there still won't be enough housing here. They are just not building, and everyone keeps having kids."

Geert, slightly balding and usually the quiet one, nodded. He was a few years older than the other men, and I knew that he had a couple of sons who were my age. He put his hands together and in a gentle voice said, "Maybe that's what it's really about, giving our children a chance at a new life. I would certainly like to know that my sons had a future with work and a place to raise families of their own."

He looked at my mother, but it was Willem who again piped up. "Well, they are certainly not going to have it in this country, buddy."

My mother sighed. "I imagine this conversation is happening in many homes these days."

She motioned for me to follow her into the kitchen and grind more coffee.

"Daddy wouldn't really think of leaving here and moving us to Australia or Canada, would he?" I asked my mother and caught the tremble in my own voice.

She was silent and stared ahead in the way that she did when she was considering the best answer to one of my questions. Then she said, "It has been hard for Daddy since he came home." She stopped and looked at me. "You know that." I nodded as she continued, "Sometimes it is just good to know that there are possibilities out there." She let out a deep sigh. "God will guide us."

I was not so sure. The world had tilted in an uncomfortable direction, but I decided to enjoy my éclair, at least for now.

## Chapter 29

# The Promise of a Mythical Land

Meanwhile, far away on the other side of the planet where summer was our winter and winter our summer, a nation was struggling with just the opposite issues from those that challenged the Dutch. In sharp contrast to our war-ravaged, depleted Netherlands, the Commonwealth of Australia, thanks largely to its woolly sheep, had experienced an economic boom during the war. Because of a shrinking population, it now faced severe labor shortages and could not sustain its new prosperity without an influx of new workers and young families.

So while the Dutch government had been urging young families to leave the country if they wanted a future, the government of postwar Australia saw the economic and military necessity to "populate or perish." It had begun a massive immigration program aimed at persuading young, healthy families from Britain, the Netherlands, and eventually other countries in Europe to leave behind their home and culture, and their wartime memories, for a fresh start in a land that promised unlimited opportunities for the future. In return for their new life, however, immigrants were expected to adopt the cultural values and language of Australia and become "New Australians," a name coined by the first minister for immigration, Arthur Calwell.

At one point it seemed to me that the topic of emigration preoccupied every adult I knew or encountered. You could not listen to the radio without hearing someone discuss emigration, and in our living room, my father and his military buddies bounced around ideas of moving to Australia, Canada, or even South Africa as if they were just thinking of going out for a beer or off to buy a pack of cigarettes.

In an effort to solve their respective problems, the Dutch and Australian governments had joined forces in an aggressive media blitz that promoted the opportunities of emigration in newspapers and on radio broadcasts. Posters and placards appeared on every available wall and pillar where I walked or rode my bicycle in Amsterdam, to announce "information meetings." People wearied by the war and frustrated by the postwar politics and economics of the Dutch government could come together and learn about the "golden opportunities" in Australia, if they were willing to take the risk.

I could not even escape the subject in the classroom at the lyceum where my history professor took it up as a social issue. He lectured that emigration was "a threat to our country because those who leave are the best kind. They are the people with courage, imagination, and entrepreneurial skills." And raising his voice, he wagged his finger at the class and almost shouted, "The countries in which these individuals settle will benefit, while the country they leave will lose the best of the gene pool."

I would always remember his words because of the intensity with which they were delivered. The class was stunned into silence, but we found our voices again when he asked us what we knew about Canada and Australia. Most of us had gleaned some background information about Canada after the Canadian troops liberated Amsterdam, but

I knew little about Australia except that it had those much talked about open spaces, weird animals with pouches, like kangaroos, and apparently lots of sheep. The professor impressed upon us that it was our responsibility to take note and observe what was happening around us because we were living in a historic time, and mass emigration was going to change the world.

"You will be living in a very different world from the one your parents grew up in," he warned us. And he would prove to be right.

After class, when a few of my classmates stopped to talk, one of the boys who always had opinions on every subject proclaimed that it might be a good thing if people left because we just did not have enough jobs or houses for everyone anyway. He then added with smug certainty, "Of course, my parents would never do that to me."

I remember that we all murmured sheepishly, "No, mine wouldn't either." But I was not so sure, and I didn't like that feeling. This is where I belonged, in this school and with my friends at the swim club in my Amsterdam. I liked it here.

I rode my bicycle home in the drizzling rain that day, and when I almost collided with another bicyclist and was yelled at, I realized that I had not been watching out for the traffic. Refocusing my attention, I was not sure if I felt angry, scared, or just plain confused and helpless. A sense of dread swept over me as I became fully aware of the fact that my future lay in my parents' hands and we might have different goals and intentions. While I had always trusted them to make the right decisions for me when I was still a little girl, I now had to struggle with my doubts.

It did not come as a surprise when my parents announced one evening that they and a couple of my dad's friends had decided to attend one of the local information meetings organized by a representative of the Australian government. I was to stay home and babysit my sister.

They returned home energized and bubbling with stories,

impressions, and a handful of colorful pamphlets that juxtaposed captions and images of the gray skies and damp weather of our Dutch lowlands with spacious rolling fields in sunny Australia. There the sun apparently always shone in a bright blue sky, the weather was always warm, and cuddly little bear-like animals called koalas nibbled away on leaves of strange-looking trees called eucalyptus.

The Australian representative had painted a glowing picture of a country with a booming economy where new immigrants, or "New Australians," could own their own home and land, my dad explained, laughing out loud when he added, "Maybe Willem was right and we could even have a horse or two."

I could hear the excitement in my father's voice. The images of acres and acres of open land under blue skies stood in stark contrast to the reality of the still boarded-up houses and crowded living conditions on the narrow, cobblestoned streets of our gray-skied Amsterdam, with its ghostly neighborhood that still reminded my father of the cruel deaths of his friends. Apparently anyone who was good with their hands could build their own house of any size in Australia. It reawakened my father's longing for freedom, usefulness, and nature that he had not expressed with such hope and joyful vigor in my presence before.

"It would be nice to live in a place where the weather is always warm and sunny," my mother said, rubbing her wrists. She then turned to me as if I were still her coconspirator of the war years. "You know, the man told us that no one ever has to be afraid of going hungry in Australia."

I knew that was a big selling point for my mother who, ever since the months of starvation that she and I had survived, still hoarded cans of food in kitchen cupboards to "guard against another famine."

We had been experiencing typical bone-chilling, damp Dutch weather. My mother had suffered from painful arthritis since the bitter months of that Hunger Winter, when thousands in our city froze and starved to death. Images of pastured sheep and munching koalas under blue skies in perpetually balmy weather clearly promised a freedom from her lingering fears and memories of the torments of cold and starvation.

In later years many emigrants would discover that the promises made by the Australian government representatives of a land of unlimited opportunity were overblown and could be judged as exploitative of the unhealed traumas and vulnerabilities of a war-wearied people, but at the time the possibility of such a land of plenty also gave a much-needed infusion of hope and energy.

But while I listened to my parents' enthusiasm, my throat tightened, and I couldn't breathe. An old familiar coughing spasm caught me unawares. "You are not thinking of moving there!" I spluttered and choked.

My mother sighed and went to the kitchen to fetch me a glass of water.

"Hey, that's not for you to worry your young head about," my dad said when I had calmed down a bit. Standing next to my chair, he looked down at me, patted my head, and ruffled my hair. "Leave the worrying to us adults. You just concentrate on your school studies and have fun swimming. Enjoy yourself." He then grinned and added, "You can't be a swimming champion if you spend your time worrying about what's going to happen in the future."

It was the first time that my dad had used the word *champion* in the context of my competitive swimming, and I was thrilled. I decided to interpret his message about not worrying to mean that emigration was just a topic of interest to my parents, not something they would act on but something to discuss and explore the way they always analyzed the news, the books they read, or the moves in the games of chess they played. I did not need to take it seriously.

Besides, my father was right. My swimming suffered if I did not focus.

One of my teammates whom I consistently beat had raced ahead of me a few days earlier in a trial for an important competition.

The coach had admonished me, "You're not focused on your stroke. What's going on?"

I realized that my mind had not been paying attention to the movements of my body in the water but was busy creating a tale for my little sister, who clamored for my stories, about a little koala bear that was forced to leave his eucalyptus tree because it was being chopped down. Yes, I really needed to focus.

During the next few months, my dad and his friends continued to meet at our home where they pored over the spread-out maps, leaflets, and newspaper articles that now covered our dining room table. Engaged in endless discussions about the broader political and economic conditions of countries that were actively seeking workers and the challenges in our own country, they drank coffee, filled the living room with their cigarette smoke, and explored their options and limitations.

But while an amazing number of young Dutch families were actually willing to take the risk of leaving everything familiar for a better life for their children on the other side of the world, most of them did not have the financial resources to pay the expensive fares for the six-week sea journey and still retain a little money, a small cushion on which to start their new life. In a last-ditch aggressive push to persuade these would-be emigrants, the governments of the Netherlands and the Commonwealth of Australia linked arms once again. They created an incentive that offered financial assistance for the cost of the journey, but in return the Australian government required the head of each immigrant household to sign a work contract for a minimum of one to two years. The Dutch government on its part stipulated that each family was only allowed to take a certain amount of money out of the Netherlands. The amount was minimal.

Many a night in the weeks that followed, I would fall asleep to the sound of my parents' low-toned voices deep in discussion about the pros and cons of leaving Holland and the serious financial and emotional costs of such a decision. I was certain that my fiercely independent father would never accept financial help and that my parents, who had struggled to pay for my books and other school expenses, probably did not have enough money to cover the exorbitant fare, so in blissful denial I decided that my parents would eventually come to their senses and see things my way.

I began to spend less and less time at home with my parents. Although my dad still helped me with my homework, he seemed lost in his own thoughts around me as he lit yet another cigarette from the one that was still between his lips. I increasingly turned to my classmates and teachers for help with and information about my schoolwork.

My mother, for her part, spent more time engrossed in conversations with friends and neighbors about their children's futures, heart-to-heart talks from which I was excluded, especially after one of the young women in our neighborhood had "an attack of nerves" and ran screaming down the street half naked. A young mother who, with her three children and a husband who had been unable to find work, lived in a cramped apartment with his parents, she had discovered she was pregnant again. The neighborhood women, including my mother, rallied around her and formed a female circle that excluded the men and us children, but as children will, we picked up the rumors and heard whispered words about finding "a good doctor."

And when I asked my mother a few weeks later how our neighbor was doing, my mom replied, "She is fine. The pregnancy has gone away."

I did not know that pregnancies could "go away," but when I tried to ask my mother more about that, she told me to stop asking questions and said, "That poor woman needs a home of her own, not another baby. Sometimes a pregnancy just does not work." She made it clear that was the end of our discussion.

Not being included in my parents' adult discussions had the advantage of perpetuating my chosen state of denial. I convinced myself with childlike confidence that ultimately my parents would never ask me to leave my school and my friends. And as an added means of self-protection, I stayed away from home as much as I could and spent my time either in the swimming pool training for the races I had entered and hoped to win, or on very long bike rides outside the city exploring the Dutch polders with my friends from school. My parents did not seem to notice my absence.

# Chapter 30

# Tsunami

But my denial did not bring about the desired result. It seldom does. In a historic phenomenon of epic proportions, the massive wave of post–World War II emigration swept up my parents along with thousands of my countrymen and women who would end up on the shores of the promised land of opportunity on the other side of the planet.

Buoyed by the promise of a fresh start and a new life far away from the memories and struggles of war and its aftermath, my father and mother sat me down in the living room one Saturday afternoon in the spring of 1950 and informed me that they had made the decision to move our family of four to Australia. If everything went according to plan, we would leave our home on the narrow cobblestoned street in Amsterdam where I had lived since I was born and board the ocean liner MS *Johan van Oldenbarneveldt* that would take us through the Mediterranean Sea, the Suez Canal to the Red Sea, and across the Indian Ocean to that new life by the end of the year.

I could not believe them. I refused to believe them. How could they possibly imagine it? "No, no, you can't do this to me! You can't make me leave my friends. My school. My swimming. No!" I responded with screams and sobs while I shook both my fists in the air at my dad as if I could force him by the power of my will to take back his words and change his mind.

My dad tried to calm me. "Henny, there are swimming pools and schools in Australia also, and you are young enough to make new friends." And he then reminded me that we had almost a whole year to prepare for our departure, and I should make the most of that time and stop being so dramatic.

I decided in that moment that I would hate my father forever, and in the weeks that followed, I sought solace for my miserable misfortune with my pals in the pool. My friends tried to cheer me up by telling me that it sounded like "a great adventure." They promised me they would write, of course, and we would all be "friends forever." My swimming coach assured me further that she had heard Australia had wonderful swim clubs and she was certain that she would hear about my winning competitions over there. "Remember, though," she said, "no matter where you go, you will always be a girl from Amsterdam. We saw you first."

In the meantime, the process of dismantling our life had begun. My parents were preoccupied with selling our furniture and figuring out their finances. The fare to Australia for the four of us presented a formidable challenge. Since his return home after the war, my dad had only been able to earn enough money to provide for our housing, our food, and my schooling. Forget about any savings. My mother stressed upon me that we would have to make decisions about what we could take with us. She planned to bring mostly objects that held emotional value.

"After all," she said with a laugh at one point, "your grandma always told us that we have gypsy blood somewhere in our ancestry."

To which my father replied that he had always admired nomads and added, "It is good to travel light."

I was not sure what he meant by that, but it would become his mantra for the rest of his life, and later in life I would be guilty of unthinkingly passing it along to my children also and telling them, "It is good to travel light."

Perhaps we needed that mantra to stay strong in the daunting task of taking apart our household. Strangers walked out the door with objects that had been part of my surroundings for as long as I could remember. I felt as if bits and pieces of the family life that had created my identity were being ripped away, leaving only fragments. A cousin took my favorite white ceramic cat lamp with the lopsided shade; a neighbor came to collect the bookcases my father had built, while another person bid on the tables and chairs in our dining room. I felt embarrassed to see my parents haggle to get the most for their furniture but relieved when my father told me that my bed would go to a family member who would not pick it up until the day we left. In the end only my mother's china, cutlery, some personal belongings, and our clothes would be shipped to Sydney and forwarded to our final destination.

For the most part, I was not too attached to our furniture, but when I realized that the move involved the sale of my dad's car and also the letting go of all our bicycles, the enormity and horror of landing in a new country without any of our possessions hit me with sharp-edged clarity. "We will be poor. We will have nothing!" I confronted my mother aghast.

She responded to my horror with her usual matter-of-fact response. "Henny, they are just material things. We can always get new bicycles. Even a car in time."

But I was not so easily appeased when I heard that my dad had sold his photography equipment including his camera. Our little camera! The tears were real when I cried out to my mother, "How could he do that? That belonged to us. We have always shared that. He and I! He should have asked me!"

She replied with a weary sigh, "We need the money to pay for the passage to Australia."

"Oh, Australia, stupid Australia, who cares? I don't want to go there anyway!" I ran into my bedroom, slammed the door behind me, and threw myself facedown onto my bed, tears soaking the covers.

In my adolescent preoccupation with my own grief, I stayed stubbornly unaware that I was not the only one emotionally distraught. Our whole family was dealing with the impact of the huge decision to leave behind everything familiar for an unknown future on the other side of the planet. As he sorted through the family belongings to decide what we could bring on board the ship, my dad announced brusquely that we were limited to a crate of belongings that measured one cubic meter. I could definitely not bring all the dolls, books, and stuffed toys I had planned to.

"But my dolls shared my tea parties when you weren't here. I can't leave them behind," I cried, pleading with him.

He relented and told me I could bring my favorite dolls, but added, "Henny, you are thirteen years old now and certainly do not need all those stuffed animals anymore." He looked at me with impatience. "There are little kids who don't have any toys. You need to learn to give things away."

Bristling with anger at my father, I started to put old toys, books, and finally my stack of stuffed animals in the bags my mother brought to me, until two tiny toy dogs, one beige in good condition, the other a faded red, its coat torn and straw stuffing all but gone, remained.

"Don't you want to keep that one?" my mom said softly.

She pointed to the faded red remnant of the little war dog I once envisioned as a wolf that could protect my father from harm. It had meant everything to me that he had kept it with him throughout his prisoner-of-war years and brought it back, a symbol of our father-daughter bond, but now I persuaded myself that I didn't care.

"You heard Daddy. He told me I couldn't take any." I scowled at my mother.

"I don't think he meant that one," she replied quietly and put it with the beige twin and the dolls I was taking.

"Why not?" I raised my voice. "It's just a squashed nothing. It's stupid. You can't even see that it was red or that it is a dog anymore."

"I think you should keep it," my mother said.

"Why?" I said with escalating scorn. "He got rid of our camera and the enlarger and all the things he and I could do together when we are in Australia. There will be nothing for us to share when we get there. Nothing! He just doesn't care about me at all."

"Stop it, stop it now!" Her voice raised, my mother grabbed my arm with unexpected force and glared at me, her eyes ablaze with anger. "Don't you see how hard he has been trying? Your father needs to get away. He can't breathe here."

For a moment I was shocked into silence. "It will give us all a new start, a chance for fresh beginnings," she added.

"But you don't even speak English," I said and heard the hurtful arrogance in my own voice.

At that she gave me an odd knowing look. "I know." Then she gave me the answer she had always given me to every challenge. "God will help me."

In the past I always believed her, but I was old enough now to know for a fact that my mother did not have an ear for foreign languages. I had been studying both French and English for several years at school, but it was my father to whom I regularly turned for help when I needed to practice words and phrases out loud. My mother got hopelessly lost in even the simplest foreign sentence, but then I also recognized that, as always, she would tackle the challenge with her usual indomitable faith and determination. That's just who she was.

# Chapter 31

# Saying Goodbyes

Having made up their minds to emigrate, my parents embarked on the process of sharing their decision and saying our good-byes to family and friends. We had already made tearful visits to aunts, uncles, and cousins in Rotterdam and The Hague and now focused on those closer by. A couple of family members had questioned the wisdom of my parents' decision, while others said that they themselves were considering emigration and might follow us, maybe soon. We would be missed, and of course everyone promised to write. And one uncle admonished me to be sure to "find and marry a nice Dutch boy" when I got to that age. Heaven forbid I should marry an Australian!

My parents had also notified my school, and it had been arranged that I would say goodbye to my classmates during a small gathering on my last day of attendance. However, on the morning that I was to say goodbye to my class, I woke up with a raging fever and a harsh chest cough. I desperately wanted to go to school. It would be my very last day, but my high fever made it clear that I could not get out of bed to go anywhere. Between shivers and hacking coughs, I sobbed and cried. My mother announced that she could not handle my roller-coaster emotions and had to make sure my sister did not catch my illness, and my dad stepped in.

He sat on the side of my bed, took hold of my hand, and said, "Henny, I know this is hard for you."

I took a raspy breath and glared at him. He sat quietly for a while and then asked me in a low serious voice, "How would you like me to go to your school and tell your classmates that you are sick and can't come as planned? I could tell them how sad you are to miss saying goodbye to them and that you sent me in your place."

I remained silent as he continued to speak. "I can be your ambassador. You can tell me what you would like me to say to them."

His words had a calming effect on my turbulent emotions, because I knew that my classmates would enjoy having my dad visit them in the classroom. He had a way with people and stories. My friends liked him, and I trusted that he would make them realize the importance of that closure for me. It would not feel like I had just walked away. I could feel my gratitude fight the anger inside of me.

"But do you have time?" I whispered in a hoarse voice as he handed me his large white handkerchief to blow my nose.

"Of course, there is always time to do the things that are really important," he replied in his gruff masculine voice.

I realized that he was handing me a gift that conveyed his love for me. Having already sold his automobile and our bicycles, he would have to take two tramcars to my school and spend his precious time there to meet with my professor and classmates. The preparations for our huge move to Australia demanded all his reserves of time and energy. If I accepted his offer, did that mean I had forgiven him for taking me away from my life in Amsterdam? I didn't want to forgive him, but I also wanted him to tell my classmates that I was sick and had not just decided not to turn up. I hesitated while he sat patiently at the edge of my bed, and then I slowly nodded.

He squeezed my hand and, as promised, made his way to the lyceum in the southern part of our city. Returning several hours later with gifts, notes, and stories, he assured me, "It felt good to be your ambassador," and told me bits and pieces of the conversations that he had with my professor and the students. "You are a bit of a heroine to your classmates. Did you know that?" he asked, and added with a conspiratorial grin, "I think some of them were actually a little jealous that they are not going to Australia."

Sick as I felt with the fever and cough that had set in, I had to admit that a little excitement had crept into my sullen mood.

"Such an adventure, you are so lucky," some of my swimming friends had said to me in the locker room after our last swim meet. "Wish my parents were as adventurous as yours. We'll probably just be stuck here in the same place for the rest of our lives. My parents never want to go anywhere."

I looked up at the weary-faced man sitting on the edge of my bed, and I recognized how deeply he cared. His visit to my school had helped me with a sense of closure with my classmates, but more importantly, it had brought me closer to him again and given the rift between us a chance to heal. I sniffled and conceded, "It will be an adventure."

He smiled and nodded. "That's my brave girl."

For a moment I flashed back to the images, so many years ago, of my father standing behind the barbed-wire fence where I could not reach him, and of the German guard to whom I had handed the little toy dog and stressed the importance that it be given to my father. The German guard did not know that the tiny red stuffed dog could change into a wolf and save my dad's life. But my dad and I had both known its magic. Yes, I was still his brave girl, and he was still the daddy I loved desperately.

Our emotional roller coaster ride was not done with us though, because soon it came time for the hardest family goodbye yet. We had to let go of our dog, Beertje. Australian quarantine laws at the time quashed any thought or attempt to bring him. Fortunately, Beertje had always been the kind of dog that made friends with everyone who patted or stroked him, and his new home would be with a family whose children he already knew and loved to play with. My father also reminded me that the same moon we saw in Amsterdam also appeared in Australia's night sky, even though at a different time.

"So," he said, "when we see the full moon in Australia, you will be able to imagine Beertje howling at it here."

His words made the other side of the world seem a little less alien and far away. I could always look up at the night sky and see the moon that drew the ancestral wildness out of our sweet house pet, causing him to howl like the gray wolf that I had once imagined at my father's side. I would still be able to see the moon swell to its fullest and break through the clouds, like a miracle, as it had on that dark New Year's Eve long ago. It felt comforting to remember that the moon that had lit the way for me and my mother to walk in safety along the icy canals and arrive home before curfew was the same moon to shine its light in the darkness all over the world for all life and all human beings. The moon did not recognize all the artifical differences and barriers we humans created amongst ourselves.

My parents could not find the right words, however, to tell my four-year-old sister, Laura, that we were leaving Beertje behind for good. Since her birth, my little sister had never been apart from our sweet family mutt. Not having any siblings close to her own age, she claimed Beertje as her best buddy and the playmate with whom she spent much of her time. They curled up on the living room floor with her arms thrown around his scruffy neck. She leaned against him seated on the back steps as they shared her child's-eye view of the world, and she showed him how to pose for the camera when my father took their picture.

In a misguided attempt to make her parting from him less painful and in the belief that she would forget about him on the long sea journey to Australia, they told her that Beertje was just staying with our friends for a while and would follow us after some time on a separate boat just for dogs, a "dog boat." It was a mistake. My sister would not forget her furry friend and would await the "dog boat" that never arrived.

But I don't think that any of us were really ready to say goodbye to Beertje permanently when, after we finished patting, stroking, and kissing him, he looked up at his new owner and walked away from us, his brown tail wagging, without so much as a backward glance. I always liked to believe that his dog nature instinctively let him know that he would be very much loved and live to the venerable old age in dog years that he actually did with the family we had chosen for him.

*My little sister, Laura, with Beertje—June 1948*

# Chapter 32

# A Sovereign Woman

W e still had to make one final farewell, however, my mother informed me, and it involved just the two of us once again.

"You and I need to do this together," she said, her tone of voice communicating the seriousness of her intent.

When I questioned her, she insisted, "I think it is important for you to be there with me," and she made it clear she had not invited my dad to join us, nor did she intend to.

And so on a typical gray Amsterdam fall morning, a damp drizzle moistening the air, I joined my mother as we retraced our steps on a familiar route through the old working-class neighborhood. We walked along the long narrow street where, in the darkest days of the Hunger Winter, the black market had flourished. I remembered that at that time men and women had lined this street in the hope of bartering their goods at exorbitant prices to desperate starving men and women. How different everything looked now. My mother and I were well fed, and everyone in the city was free and safe to come and go as they pleased. With the exception of a few bicyclists and a group of small children playing hopscotch, the street seemed almost empty.

No German soldiers threatened our way with a "Heil Hitler" salute or a "Halt" with its menacing demand to see our identity papers. We had no big secrets to hide this time, and yet as we walked in silence, I had a vague awareness of the presence of fear and the constant vigilance that, like a protective raincoat slung over one's arm on a sunny day, was ready to be donned at a moment's notice. My mother and I made our way across a narrow bridge and walked a distance along the canal on the other side until we reached the small familiar store. When we walked in through the glassed-in front door, an overpowering fragrance of cigars and pipe tobacco plunged me back into a time when I had been only half the age I was now. The last time I had come here with my mother had been before the Nazis broke into our home in the middle of the night and took Nel.

For a brief moment I experienced myself in the perplexing sensation of two overlapping realities. I knew that I was standing in the tobacco store, but I also saw Nel being dragged across the floor, saw the pistol being pointed at my mother's head when I could only watch. My heart thumped with a hard beat against my ribs, making it difficult to breathe. My vision blurred. I wanted to cling to my mother. Yet at the same time I was aware that I was standing in the tobacco store and that I was bigger and older now. I blinked and saw only the boxes of cigars and tobacco displays on a glass counter. We were safe. I took a slow, deep breath.

Almost immediately, Mr. V, looking a little more robust than I remembered him, appeared from the back of the shop and greeted my mother with the kind of affection that only comes from a deep mutual respect. Then he held out his hand to me, told me that I had grown into "quite a young lady," and asked if I still saved cigar bands. Surprised that he remembered, I had to tell him that I did not, but yes, I still had the album of my collection from the time when both Mr. Sleumer and Nel had been with us.

He smiled and turned to my mother. Soothed by his calming

voice, I sat on a chair as I took in the familiar sight of boxes and boxes of cigars and noticed the new assortment of colorful bands in different shapes and sizes. I listened and half drifted to the sound of Mr. V's and my mother's words as they entered into conversation and exchanged memories. They sounded much like the seasoned veterans of war who had met with my father in the living room of our home. Perhaps it was the inhalation of the intoxicating tobacco smells, or maybe the memories that had been triggered, but at some point I began to see my mother as if through a different set of eyes. The woman engaged in conversation with Mr. V transformed into more than just my mother, more than the woman who cooked our family meals, cared for our home, and took care of my sister and me when we were sick. I saw a woman who was more than my dad's wife and companion or the woman who served coffee and pastries to his friends, even more than the mother who so proudly let me pat her belly when she was growing my little sister inside of her, and I was allowed to feel the baby kick.

I had started menstruating three years after my sister was born. "You are a woman now," my mother and aunts had whispered, and my body's new status and the mystery of "being a woman" came with warnings about boys and men, the clothes I wore, and stories about girls who had faced tragedies because of unwanted pregnancies. Having turned from girl into woman after I had that first period, everything about me had suddenly seemed to focus on the dangers of my body with its breasts, its bleeding, and its potential for babies. But I had seen my mother and Nel face the Nazi thugs in our living room when I was just a little girl. As I now watched my mother deeply involved in a mutual recognition with Mr. V, two secret warriors, male and female, meeting in equal regard and respect, I was granted a glimpse into the complexity of womanhood that my culture had not yet acknowledged. At that moment in that little cigar store, the image of the woman I wanted to become, like an image on the photographic paper in my father's darkroom, began to take shape somewhere deep inside of me.

I heard my mother ask about Nel, whom we had not seen for a long time.

"No," Mr. V told my mother, he unfortunately did not have a forwarding address for her either.

"Let it be," he added. "Everyone needs to get on with their own lives. Go make a new life with your family. Leave the past here. The war is over."

"Will it ever really be?" my mother asked softly in a voice that held all the unspoken pain that still lived inside her.

I watched her eyes flood with tears when they said their final goodbyes, and she and I walked away from that little tobacco store. One day as an adult woman, I would return to Amsterdam and look for that little store again, but I would not be able to find it. However, no matter what my age, when I close my eyes, it is always there with Mr. V behind the counter risking his life as he passes my mother the fake ration coupons that fed my secret stepsister. They both reside in that sacred place, the inner sanctuary of my memory, where people never grow old.

"He was a good man, a very courageous man," my mother whispered as she took hold of my arm. Arm in arm, in silent reverie, she and I slowly walked the familiar route home one last time.

As if all our history had already been erased, our home felt empty when we arrived there. All our goodbyes had been said, including to our neighbors. The few belongings that would accompany us had already been picked up for shipping, and not much was left to take care of.

Having been fully approved by the Australian government, our only remaining task was to pick up our passports and official emigration papers from the office of the Dutch Emigration Department. My parents decided to leave my little sister with one of my aunts for the occasion, but they thought it was important for me to be included in the process, which I liked because it made me feel like a grown-up. When we arrived at the emigration office, we were given chairs that faced the Dutch consul who sat behind a desk that I would always remember as enormous. A not-quite-middle-aged man, dressed in an immaculate dark gray suit, white shirt, and somber tie, he took his time to look over our papers. In a monotone voice, he asked my father a few questions and, seemingly satisfied with the answers, motioned him with a wave of his hand to get up and approach the desk so that he could give my dad his passport. He waited for my dad to return to his chair and opened my mother's passport. He looked at her with a questioning look on his face, stared down at the papers before him, and glanced up at her again, as if studying her face. There was an awkward silence in the room. He seemed to ponder something for a moment before he slowly rose out of his chair and with deliberate steps strode around the large desk toward my mother.

"What is he doing?" my mother asked, her voice trembling. "What is wrong now?"

Assuming a formal bow, the stern-faced official bent down to my mother and asked, "Mrs. de Vries, may I shake your hand? It would be such an honor."

With a perplexed shrug of her shoulder, my mother nodded and let him take her hand. He squatted down before her so that they were at eye level and spoke on in a voice resonating respect. "I want you to know that it is an honor for me to shake your hand. I want to thank you. You make me proud of my country. You make me proud to be Dutch."

Whereupon he straightened up, walked back to his desk, and picked up a passport and a typewritten certificate that he placed in my mother's hand. The small official "certificate" was a copy of a brief letter that had been sent to the Australian Legation in The Hague whose job it was to ensure that prospective emigrants to Australia, especially women, were of good moral character. An official record and recognition of my mother's "illegal work" during the Nazi occupation of Amsterdam, composed of only two small paragraphs, it declared her as "an active and bona fide resistance worker" whose "illegal work consisted of taking care of a Jewish girl." It was the first and only official recognition that my mother ever received, and I would always think of it as serendipitous that it occurred because of our emigration to Australia when we were leaving Amsterdam.

My father looked on as my mother accepted the acknowledgment from the official. I recognized the look on his face. It held the same expression of delight and pride that I had so often witnessed when he told and retold the story of how once during his cavalry days he had ridden with the queen, his much beloved Queen Wilhelmina. As the adored youngest son of a widowed single mother, he had never made a secret of his admiration for strong women. At that moment I witnessed that same admiration on his face, and, as he smiled at my mother, I had the insight that my father now had his queen at his side. It would be many years before I could articulate the thoughts that played through my mind on that day, but that recognition gave me my first inkling into the archetypal background that shapes our human relational patterns, and the image of woman as warrior and sovereign queen.

**STICHTING 1940-1945**
District Amsterdam Vondelstraat 11 E  •  Telefoon 84422  •  Giro 194045

*Bij beantwoording gelieve U onder
staande gegevens te vermelden*

AMSTERDAM,June 27th 1950

DOSSIER   8585

AFD,  Onderz/DM

C E R T I F I C A T E

in behalf of the Australian Legation
The Hague

We herewith declare that Mrs. de VRIES-
HESSELMAN, born March 13th 1911, is registered as an active and bonafide resistance-
worker.
Her illegal work consents in taking care of a
jewish girl, who she housed and for which
the illegal people gave money and ration-cards
By treason this jewish girl later on was
taken from home during the night.

Stichting 1940-1945
Amsterdam-District

For the Direction

# Chapter 33

# Leaving Amsterdam

A nd so on December 14, 1950, less than three months after my thirteenth birthday, my parents, my little sister, and I found ourselves standing on the deck of the large Dutch ocean liner, the MS *Johan van Oldenbarneveldt*, which had been especially refitted for the immigrant trade to carry twice the number of its original passengers to the other side of the world. My body pressed hard against the cold railing, I leaned forward as far as I could to wave goodbye to a group of girls who had gathered on the dock. They were holding up a large banner that displayed the white letters *ADZ* against a black-and-red background. The letters stood for the Amsterdamse Dames Zwemclub (Amsterdam Ladies Swim Club), the logo of our swim club and team that I had worn with pride on my swimsuit in my trainings and competitions. My swimming pals had come to send me off to my new life in Australia. I waved to them with the biggest, most energetic arm movements I could muster, as the ship slowly began to pull away from the land of my birth. I leaned harder into the railing until a gap of dark water appeared between the ship and the dock where they stood. They kept the banner aloft and I continued to wave. The chasm of water widened between us and then widened some more. My friends became smaller and smaller until they were no more than Lilliputian figures in a faraway distance. Then abruptly, as if they were never there, they were lost to my sight.

The cold winter wind pelted a sleety rain onto my face that absorbed the tears I could not control. I stopped waving and dropped my right hand, but my left hand clutched a book to my chest. A parting gift inscribed and signed by fifteen of my swim mates, it was a young adult Dutch novel that bore the title *Hup Puck . . . !* (Rough translation: *Go for It, Puck . . . !*) It told the story of a young Dutch swimmer who becomes a swim champion and comes of age at the newspaper where she works and meets the newspaperman she will marry. The gift would prove to be a prophetic foreshadowing of my future destiny, but that is the Australian part of my story.

The ship pulled away from the harbor. I turned around to face my parents, my mother's penetrating gaze meeting mine, my father balancing my restless little sister up on his arms so she would not fall overboard. I nodded my silent affirmation. *Yes, I could do this.* After all, I was my mother's daughter.

Our little family of four turned our backs to the past and walked into the main lounge of the ship that would carry us to our new life, but I made a promise to myself that I would find a way to return one day.

## Permission to reprint:

I wish to thank, Nancy Cater, editor of *Spring*, for her kind permission to reprint the segments of my memoir that appeared originally in "Beyond Forgiveness: Re-Weaving the Remains of War," *The Psychology of Violence*. Spring Vol. 81: A Journal of Archetype and Culture, Spring 2009, 225–241.

# Acknowledgments

This book has been gnawing at me for decades, but I always hesitated. Writing a memoir about my childhood under Nazi tyranny felt somewhat self-indulgent. After all, I survived to live a long and richly textured life, while so many others suffered unspeakable tortures and died cruel deaths. But when I saw torch-bearing neo-Nazis with swastikas on my television screen this year, and I heard our president and his right-wing supporters threaten women's reproductive rights while dismissing their stories of sexual abuse and harassment, I realized I had a moral obligation. Those of us who have witnessed how hard-fought freedoms can be eroded and reversed at lightning speed, and have experienced how bigotry, fear, and hatred can be manipulated to incite mass brutality and slaughter, owe it to future generations to tell our stories.

Still, this book would not have come about if I had not been supported, urged on, and encouraged to put down words by a large number of people. I want to first express my gratitude to all those I do not individually mention by name. The friends and colleagues who heard anecdotal fragments of my story over the years and kept urging me to write the book; the students and clients who shared and transformed their own experiences of trauma and dark shadows in class or in our therapy room. Your courageous willingness to be open and vulnerable showed me the healing power at the depths of our collective stories and inspired me to tell mine.

I am deeply grateful to my one and only sister, Laura de Vries, for her love, encouragement, and permission to share our family story and include the parts that strictly belong to her. When I asked her to read the raw chapters that I sent her willy-nilly at random, she gently received each one and, without critique, as a mother receives a child's first attempts, put them in a binder and encouraged me to keep writing. Without my sister's loyal, generous heart with its supportive nudges, I can honestly say that this book would not have been written.

My big blessing in life is my three children Laura, Grant, and Susanne Oliphant. How can I even begin to acknowledge them fully? My story contains the mother-line seeds of their individual life stories. They carry the trans-generational history of World War II in their flesh and bones, in whispered memories and grandparents' hushed silences and warnings, in the cupboards of our kitchen that could never be empty of cans of food "in case of another famine," and, most important, in the way all three of them stand for moral courage and the defense of human freedom, rights, and dignity. From the time they were little kids clamoring for my bedtime stories, till now that they are adults I admire and respect, each one gave me the physical and emotional prodding and support to tell the whole story and publish the book. They literally are the breath that gave it life. And I must give a special bow to my younger daughter, Susanne, for holding my feet to the fire, as I complained and argued, until the right title for my book finally emerged.

I am deeply grateful to my Dutch cousins still living in the Netherlands: Cor Leibbrand, Netty Aschman-Pley, and Hanny

Nieuwburg Hasselman. They and their families carry their own memories and personal legacies of that horrific time, and each one graciously read my first, unedited draft and urged me to get the manuscript published. Cor Leibbrand and I played as children in Amsterdam, neither of us realizing that we grew up with similar fears and experiences that we never shared. I thank Cor, for naming our innocent silence the "code of silence that hid our fears." I struggled to express the authentic voice of the little girl who experienced the events I write about, and I wish to thank my cousin Netty Aschman-Pley, who, six years older than I, embraced me and affirmed with empathy in her voice that she did indeed remember "that little girl." And a special thanks goes to Netty's daughter, Loura Pley, who took the time to not only read my manuscript but also send me relevant links to Dutch media that affirmed that the stories told by witness-es and survivors continue to be of importance. I did my best to check personal memories against family stories and letters, and I am deeply grateful to Hanny Nieuwburg Hasselman, the daughter of my mother's beloved brother, my gentle uncle Dick, for sharing the wartime letters that my mother had written to my grandmother and uncle during the Hunger Winter. Reading my mother's words, in her familiar graceful script—words of love and concern for her own mother and brother and a desperate wish for peace in the year ahead—amplified my mother's voice and deepened her authentic presence in my memoir.

I owe a great debt to the therapeutic community of Santa Barbara where I met teachers, supervisors, future colleagues, and lifelong friends who taught me the healing power and collective value of sharing our individual life stories. In particular I want to name: Mary Leibman, Kate Smith-Hanssen, Karen Perrino, Suzanne Hamilton, and Serena Carroll, extraordinary women who for thirty or more years have held me in an embrace of female nurture and energy that gave me the cour-age to step back, explore, and retell the memories of the war child. Mary

Leibman, who personifies wisdom, elegance, and grace, has supported my career, my family, and my writing with a boundless generosity of heart, intelligence, and soul. Her unflinching demand for total honesty and authenticity in friendship has taught me the true meaning of having and being a "best friend." Kate Smith-Hanssen, with her depth of knowledge in archetypal psychology and mythology, helped me clarify the cultural and archetypal patterns of "fathers' daughters" and "mothers' daughters." Our long conversations, as we traveled the world and taught and led workshops together, deepened my understanding of what it means to be a "mother's daughter" in a patriarchal culture. Karen Perrino provided the nurturing space where I could process raw, unfiltered emotions until they could be shaped into words. In my desire to become a therapist who could help others deal with unresolved trauma, I was forced to address my own childhood experiences. For many years Karen's home became the sanctuary where I sought refuge, no matter where she lived at the time. From Suzanne Hamilton, my fellow midlife classmate in the study of psychology, I learned about the similarities between American Midwestern common sense and Dutch practicality. With her wry wit and experience in Jungian analysis, we honored our dreams while sharing an irreverent mix of Kansas-Dutch humor that helped me navigate my serious midlife transition with sometimes-ironic gleefulness. Serena Carroll, my mystical friend, whose astrological wisdom has expanded my universe through her writings on the planetary influences on our life patterns, has "had my back" when I most needed it and continues to inspire me to read the stars and tell my stories.

A special note of credit goes to the first friend I made in Santa Barbara, Ann MacNair Shaw. Ann helped me buy my first computer over thirty years ago. She took my author picture for this book, restored the old family photos that are included, set up my website, and is always there to calm me when technology short-circuits my brain.

I bow in admiration and respect to my author friends Patricia Reis and Maureen Murdock for the authentic voice and deep wisdom they continue to express in the numerous books they have written and published. The generous sharing of their writing and publishing experiences provided me with invaluable guidance to cross this new threshold.

This book could not have been written if it were not for the years of deep analysis with Jungian analysts Dr. Kurt Goerwitz and Dr. Claire Douglas. Each in their own caring but professional approach helped me analyze and transform the war-related images that plagued my dreams. They patiently provided the container for the emotions and repetitive fragments of my story, until it was fully told. I am especially grateful for their superb clinical skills that helped me claim my separate identity from that of my mother, without damaging my access to the fierce internalized mother whose strength, faith, and courage continues to inspire and guide my life's path.

And in memoriam I need to name Jungian analysts Helen Luke, Marion Woodman, and Sonny Herman who, in my work with them, helped me transform the obstacles on the psychological journey. Each in their individual way helped me find my voice. They remain inner guides.

My years of teaching at Pacifica Graduate Institute gave me the opportunity to share reflections, thoughts, and anecdotes from my life story in lectures and presentations. I am grateful to Dr. Steve Aizenstat and Maren Hansen for sharing their visionary dreams, when I had joined them on a journey to visit the sacred sites of ancient gods and goddesses in Greece and Turkey. Steve's vision for an institute of psychological learning that included the world soul and Maren's spiritual passion and our mutual background in theology inspired me to move to Santa Barbara for two years to pursue a master's degree in psychology. I never left.

The Santa Barbara Writers Conference with its range of wonderful speakers and teachers gave me a chance to hear others' life stories and put my own in writing. I owe special thanks to Susan Miles Gulbransen, who encouraged me to enter my story "Pilgrimage" in the nonfiction writer's contest. An account of my return to Amsterdam for analytical work with Rabbi Dr. Sonny Herman, it won first-place.

And in memoriam I wish to acknowledge Lisa Lenard-Cook who helped me find a place to stand in my story.

In She Writes Press my memoir has safely landed in the capable hands of publisher Brooke Warner and the guidance of Cait Levin, and I want to thank Julie Metz for her brilliant iconic cover design. It is an amazing experience to find myself in the She Writes Press sisterhood of powerful women authors, who have reached out to me with support, insights, sound advice, and wise counsel.

And finally, I come home in love and gratitude to my husband, Harlan Green, for his encouragement and support of my writing. As a Berkeley graduate, he chose service in the Peace Corps over fighting the war in Vietnam and shares my abhorrence for violence, cruelty, and bigotry. He also writes me poetry that makes me remember the yearning for love, the desire for beauty, and the potential for goodness in the human soul.

# About the Author

© Ann MacNair Shaw

**H**endrika de Vries believes that memories hold the keys to our future. Her life experiences, from the dark days of Nazi-occupied Amsterdam as a child through her years as a swimming champion, young wife, and mother in Australia and a move to America in the sixties, have infused her work as a therapist, teacher, and writer.

A depth-oriented marriage and family therapist for over thirty years, de Vries has used memories, intuitive imagination, and dreams to heal trauma, empower women, and address life transitions and relationship issues. As adjunct faculty at Pacifica Graduate Institute, she helped students explore the archetypal patterns in their life stories.

De Vries holds a BA with Phi Beta Kappa from the University of Colorado, an MTS in theological studies from Virginia Theological Seminary, and an MA in counseling psychology from Pacifica Graduate Institute in Santa Barbara. Her published articles include: "Rediscovering Home: A Myth for Our Time," *Spring: A Journal of Archetype and Culture*; "Beyond Forgiveness: Re-Weaving the Remains of War," *Spring: A Journal of Archetype and Culture;* and "The Chrysalis Experience: A mythology for Times of Transition," *Depth Psychology: Meditations in the Field.*

Read more at www.agirlfromamsterdam.com.

# Discussion Questions

1. The author begins her book as a "daddy's girl." What do you think she means by that, and how has she changed by the time she boards the ship for Australia?

2. Why do you think the author waited until she was almost eighty before publishing the book?

3. When her father is taken away, the author "imagines" that her little toy dog becomes a wolf. How does her imagination or experience help her deal with the loss? What does the toy dog symbolize when her father returns?

4. Before her mother decides to join the resistance and shelter a Jewish girl, she takes her little daughter, Henny, to spend time with her family in Rotterdam. What is her motivation? How does that impact the mother-daughter relationship?

5. What impact does hiding a Jewish "stepsister" have on Henny's developing awareness of prejudice and the Nazi belief in ethnic superiority?

6. Throughout the book, the mother shows a strong belief in God. How does this help or motivate her to resist the Nazis? Do you think that her religious belief helps her daughter? How do you view the young daughter's unfolding relationship with God?

7. Mother and daughter form an intense bond in their struggle for survival. How does this impact the daughter's relationship with her father?

8. What do you think about the mother's answer to her brother's challenge that she should not have put her child in danger to save a stranger? He insists that as a mother the safety of her own child should have been her primary concern. How would you feel if you were faced with a similar moral choice?

9. PTSD is widely experienced by returning war veterans. Do you have personal experience with PTSD? How does it impact the family in this memoir?

10. When Henny displays symptoms of post-traumatic stress, or "war nerves" as the doctor called it, her dad buys her a puppy and makes her carry it home. The author says that she thinks this was one of the wisest actions her father took to help her heal. Why do you think that was so healing for her?

11. The book lays out both cultural and emotional post–World War II reasons for the family's decision to move to Australia. How is their decision to emigrate similar or different from immigrants today?

12. The author says that postwar Australia, in order to replenish their dwindling labor force, actively enticed European immigrants with promises of a new life in a land of opportunity. What

really, do you think, ultimately convinced the author's family to leave the Netherlands?

13. When she leaves the Netherlands, her swim mates give Henny a book as a parting gift. The book is about a champion swimmer who meets her future husband at the newspaper where she works. The author sees it as a prophetic blueprint for her future. What impact does this have on how you, the reader, may imagine her future?

14. When the family boards the ship, Henny calls herself her "mother's daughter." She has a close relationship with her father, so what does she mean? And how has her father's relationship with women helped her reach this decision?

15. What feelings and thoughts are you left with after reading this book?